The Advancing Frontier

Trudy J. Hanmer

THE ADVANCING FRONTIER

Issues in American History

Franklin Watts
New York/London/Toronto
Sydney/1986

Photographs courtesy of:
The Bettmann Archive, Inc.: pp. 17, 30, 35, 42,
76, 96, 104, 109, 112, 121, 123, 130;
Cincinnati Public Library: p. 50;
West Point Museum, U. S. Military Academy: p. 67;
Woolaroc Museum: p. 85;
Library, State Historical Society
of Colorado: p. 101.

Library of Congress Cataloging-in-Publication Data

Hanmer, Trudy J.
The advancing frontier.

(Issues in American history)
Bibliography: p.
Includes index.
Summary: Traces the history of westward expansion in
the United States discussing the evolution of the popular
idea of an unlimited frontier and its influence on
American thought.
1. United States—Territorial expansion—
Juvenile literature. 2. Frontier and pioneer life—
United States—Juvenile literature. [1. United States—
Territorial expansion. 2. Frontier and pioneer life]
I. Title. II. Series.
E179.5.H25 1986   973   86-9251
ISBN 0-531-10267-X

Copyright © 1986 by Trudy J. Hanmer
All rights reserved
Printed in the United States of America
6 5 4 3 2 1

For Emmie and Tinker

Contents

Chapter One
"Westward the Star of Empire"

11

Chapter Two
A New Nation Pushes West, 1776–1815

23

Chapter Three
Manifest Destiny: Americans Fill the Continent

45

Chapter Four
Manifest Destiny, Politics, and Civil War

63

Chapter Five
The Dark Side of Westward Expansion: Prejudice and Oppression

79

Chapter Six
*Cowboys and Miners:
The Wild, Wild West*

99

Chapter Seven
*Settling the Plains: The Closing
of the Continental Frontier*

115

Chapter Eight
*Beyond the
Continental Frontiers*

125

Chapter Nine
*The Frontier Legacy
Continues*

133

Suggestions for
Further Reading
139

Index
141

The Advancing Frontier

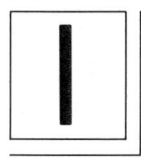

I   "Westward the Star of Empire"

In 1782 a Frenchman, Jean de Crèvecoeur, attempted to explain what it meant to be an American. In a series of essays titled *Letters from an American Farmer*, Crèvecoeur developed the theory that Americans were different from their Old World European ancestors. Something seemed to happen to people in the New World that set them apart from the people living in older, more established civilizations. In Crèvecoeur's words, "Here [in America] . . . individuals of all nations are melted into a new race of men, whose labors and posterity will one day cause great changes in the world."

Most American historians have agreed with Crèvecoeur's basic premise that Americans differed from the people from whom they descended. For two centuries, however, they have searched for reasons for the difference, particularly reasons that would provide a common denominator for the American experience. Americans come from many nations, believe in many different religions, are members of many different races—and yet they are all Americans. They share certain identifiable characteristics. Black Americans, Irish Americans, Italian Americans, and Asian Americans are easily identified by non-Americans as Americans rather than as Africans, Irish, Italians, or Asians.

The conquering of the frontier is one common denominator in the American experience that has helped to explain what it is to be an American. Almost every immigrant group that settled in the United States helped to tame the wilderness. From the landing of the Pilgrims at Plymouth, Massachusetts, in 1620 to the early years of the twentieth century, the country continually moved west. New generation after new generation, experienced the hardships and challenges of developing previously unsettled territory.

Westward expansion and the frontier are inextricably linked in the American tradition. To many non-Americans the most common image of the United States is one of a land where cowboys and Indians squared off in gun battles on unsettled plains. Where were these cowboys and Indians? Out West—or on the frontier. But the advancing frontier did not reach Hollywood's cowboy territory until late in the nineteenth century. For two hundred years the line of settlement pushed against the frontiers in the eastern half of the country. As Walt Whitman wrote in *Leaves of Grass*, the frontier began along the Atlantic coast, "Starting from fish-shape Paumanok where I was born . . ." John Quincy Adams, speaking in 1802 from another coastal town, Plymouth, Massachusetts, predicted the westward expansion of the country when he claimed, "Westward the star of empire takes its way." To Adams at the turn of the nineteenth century, Ohio and Kentucky were the frontier.

Long after Adams's time, when the land was finally settled, the idea of the frontier remained. For the first three hundred years the advancing frontier had meant, for the most part, the westward movement of civilization. In the twentieth century the advancing frontier came to be a peculiarly American concept applicable to any new challenge. As early as 1849 Henry David Thoreau wrote in *A Week on the Concord and Merrimack Rivers*, "The frontiers are not east or west, north or south, but wherever a man *fronts* a fact." With this idea firmly rooted in the American intellectual tradition, it is not surprising that Vannevar Bush, a scientist writing one hundred years later, would title his book *Science: The Endless Frontier*.

Frederick Jackson Turner and his Thesis

In the late nineteenth century, historians began to write about the importance of the frontier in American history—both the actual frontier of westward expansion and the concept of the frontier that had become a part of American thinking. The frontier, they thought, held the answer to Crèvecoeur's question. No other nation in modern times had civilized such a vast territory. Clearly, the presence of a frontier and the idea of a frontier held the key to understanding what it was to be an American.

The most famous of these historians of the late nineteenth century was Frederick Jackson Turner. In 1893 Turner, a young professor at the University of Wisconsin, delivered an address to the annual meeting of the American Historical Association. This address was destined to be reprinted countless numbers of times; the "Turner thesis" would remain throughout the twentieth century among the most controversial theories of American history. In this paper Turner hypothesized that the course of American history had been determined from the first by the nation's propensity for westward expansion. The presence of the advancing western frontier, he argued, explained the development of the American character and the adherence of Americans to democratic institutions.

The timing of Turner's address, which he titled "The Significance of the Frontier in American History," was crucial. The supervisor of the census for 1890 had declared in his analysis of the data collected in that year,

"Up to and including 1890 the country had a frontier of settlement, but at present the unsettled area has been so broken into by isolated bodies of settlement that there can hardly be said to be a frontier line . . . its westward movement . . . can not, therefore, any longer have a place in the census reports."

What the Census of 1890 meant to Turner and to many others was that the frontier could no longer advance physically within the continental United States. Furthermore, they believed that the end of the frontier meant the end of the single most important factor in determining the national character and life of the United States. As Turner put it, "The existence of an area of free land, its continuous recession, and the advance of American settlement westward, explain American development." For Turner, the frontier was defined as "the meeting point between savagery and civilization." Along each new frontier as the nation's population expanded westward, people were forced to live simple, even primitive, lives that he believed made them rethink the institutions and structure of the society they had left behind in the more civilized eastern areas. People in western localities, reasoned Turner, were more individualistic and more democratic, and thus the movement west continually strengthened such American characteristics as faith in democracy.

Turner's thesis has always been controversial. Historians have attacked his essay on a variety of grounds. Some argue that Turner's version of westward expansion holds true only for white male pioneers. Others maintain that America's democratic institutions and Constitution owe as much to the laws of England and the capitalistic economic system favored by the nation's early leaders as they do to the frontier. Still other historians have questioned Turner's emphasis on one theme as the overriding influence in American history. These historians argue that urbanization, immigration, and a host of other forces are equally as powerful as the frontier in explaining the American experience.

The Impact of the Advancing Frontier
No matter how one feels about Turner's thesis, it is undeniable that the frontier has been a powerful influence in American history. Only the continental frontier ceased to exist by the time of the Census of 1890. The pioneering of the Alaskan oil fields and the exploration of outer space illustrate that America is still pushing against frontiers. Modern American adventurers share many of the characteristics of their ancestors. For instance, Sally Ride, the first American woman to travel in space, has often been compared to the sharpshooter, Annie Oakley. This kind of comparison underlines the endurance of the frontier legacy in American thought. Whatever one believes about the extent of the frontier's impact on American history, the concept of an advancing frontier remains an important idea in the minds of most Americans. As William K. Wyant has written in *Westward in Eden*, "They have been telling us for more than a century that the frontier is no more, but we refuse to believe it." Alaska, outer space, the world of computers—each is approached by modern Americans as yet another advancing frontier.

To understand how Alaska and space and modern technology are seen as the edges of new frontiers, it is necessary to look back and identify the common American characteristics that were developed as the frontier advanced. Each decade from the American Revolution to 1900 saw the push westward. When the first census was completed in 1790, there were four million Americans, and the center of the nation, from the point of view of population, was located east of Baltimore. By 1980 the nation's two and a quarter million people were centered in Illinois.

Americans filled the continent rapidly and confidently after the United States became an independent nation. From the landings at Jamestown, Virginia, and Plymouth, Massachusetts, to the settlement of the Appalachians had taken the early pioneers over one hundred and fifty years. To settle the country between the Appalachians and the Mississippi River took only fifty years. To fill in the great expanse between the Mississippi and California took only another half century. People born in 1809, the year of Abraham Lincoln's birth, could live to visit their grandchildren on either coast by way of (relatively) comfortable railroad travel. In short, Americans as a nation believed in advancing west as fast as possible. On a personal level and as national policy, they agreed that moving west was the right thing to do.

Because the line of frontier continuously ran to the west of civilized areas, westward expansion became synonymous with conquering the wilderness or frontier. (It is important to remember that the west is not the frontier in all nations. In the Soviet Union, for example, the most highly civilized areas of the nation are in the western, European section of the country; the frontiers lie to the east and north.) Because the advancing frontier in the United States usually moved west, the idea of the western region of the nation as "wilder" than the East passed into the national consciousness and has remained there to this day.

Faced with the wild character of the frontier, the settlers sought at once to tame it. As each group of settlers moved west, they worked rapidly to re-create the civilization left behind. Pioneers during the eigh-

Artist Emmanuel Leutze romanticized the westward movement in this painting, "Westward the Course of Empire Takes Its Way," from which a frescoe in the Capitol building in Washington, D.C. was made.

teenth, nineteenth, and early twentieth centuries may have wanted to escape the crowding of the eastern seaboard, but they did not seek "to get away from it all" in the modern sense of that phrase. As quickly as possible they wanted technology, markets, commerce—in short urbanization—to catch up with them. Whether they sought land or fortunes in furs and metal, they needed contact with civilization to realize their economic profit. As Horace Greeley exhorted his readers in 1855, "Turn your face to the great West, and there build up a home and fortune."

The contact between the frontier and the settlers helped forge characteristics that we have come to identify as "American," characteristics that are both good and bad. The pioneers were rugged, optimistic, democratic, and hardy. On the other hand, these people were often nationalistic, racist, expedient, wasteful, and materialistic. They carried the American flag with them and believed it to be the divine right of the United States to stretch "from sea to shining sea." The native inhabitants of the land, the Indians, were tolerated as neighbors in the earliest years when wresting civilization from the forest necessitated accepting help from anyone, even those they considered "savages." As soon as towns grew up, with their churches and neighborhoods, old prejudices quickly returned.

Not surprisingly, the Native Americans hold a different memory of the advancing frontier. In 1933 a Sioux chief, Luther Standing Bear, wrote in *Land of the Spotted Eagle*,

> Only to the white man was nature "a wilderness" and only to him was the land "infested" with "wild" animals and "savage" people. To us it was tame. . . . Not until the hairy man

from the east came and with brutal frenzy heaped his injustices upon us and the families we loved was it "wild" for us. When the very animals of the forest began fleeing from his approach, then it was that for us the "Wild West" began.

In advancing the frontier a majority inevitably imposed its will on a minority. This happened not only in the case of Native Americans, but also with other minority ethnic and religious groups. The tensions between the majority and the minorities helped forge a practical democracy time and time again. The result along each border of the frontier was the creation of institutions more democratic than the Old World had ever seen.

Because limitless land seemed to be there for the taking, the history of westward expansion often seems colored as much by greed, corruption, and waste as by high-minded virtues. In praising the settlers in his poem "Pioneers! O Pioneers!" Walt Whitman charges, "get your weapons ready,/Have you your pistols? have you your sharp-edged axes?" The guns destroyed the animals; the axes destroyed the forests. Government giveaways of federal land led eventually to the environmental problems of the twentieth century. For the pioneers of nearly three centuries, however, the frontier had meant that there were always more animals and there was always more land.

The advancing frontier seems always to have been peopled by characters who typified America in the extreme. Daniel Boone, Kit Carson, and Calamity Jane lived in different eras, yet they have tended to merge in the national consciousness and in legend as having belonged to the same band of pioneers. They exhibited characteristics that are not only western, but American. They were bold, adventuresome, strong, honest, brash, forceful, reliable, hardworking, daring, exuberant, and larger than life. In the words of the patriotic poet Edgar Guest, the frontier people shared

> A blending of wisdom and daring . . .
> A bit of the man who has neighbored with
>   mountains and forests and streams
> A touch of the man who has labored
> To model and fashion his dreams . . .

Over the years ordinary citizens have looked to the pioneer and western hero to define the true American.

The frontier peopled by these heroes was located in different places with each step of its advancement. To the Revolutionary War veteran, the West was the area around Fort Pitt, soon to become the settlement of Pittsburgh. To the Carolina planter, it was the rich farmland of Alabama. To Tom Lincoln, father of Abraham, it was first Kentucky and finally Illinois. To the gold-hungry miner, the West changed rapidly: from California in 1849, to Colorado in 1859, with a stop in Nevada along the way. To countless Scandinavian immigrants the frontier was the unbroken plain of high grass spreading from the Mississippi to the Rocky Mountains. And to the Irish worker, the West meant the outermost path of the rail lines he helped to lay across the nation in the 1860s and 1870s. There is a tendency, as Robert Riegel explains in *America Moves West*, to see the frontier or the West ". . . as a magic word with which to conjure alluring pictures of an open, wind-swept plain over which roamed bold and romantic riders. . . . The West appear(s) a land of freedom, where a man was his own master, bold and self-reliant, meeting human and physical hardships with heroic bravery."

The Enduring Legacy of the Frontier
Whether or not the advancing frontier created the historical impact that Turner attributed to it, there can be no doubt that the rapid populating of the continental United States made a significant impression on the minds of Americans, an impression that has yet to fade. Americans often act as though the frontier is still there. At some point or other we like to believe that there is a little bit of the pioneer left in each of us.

As a nation we value democracy, individualism, strength, freedom, inventiveness, private ownership, free enterprise, and a sense of adventure. While it might be argued that all of those qualities were present in some form in the earliest explorers and settlers who came to the Atlantic Coast, it is certainly true that they were kept alive by succeeding generations of western migrants. And, in the final analysis, this may be the greatest legacy of the frontier.

Unlike other new nations that were formed in small spaces captured from another people, the United States lay adjacent to a vast, underpopulated expanse when its citizens undertook to shape the nation from the continent. It took a century after independence to fill the continent with people. In the course of that process, the traits that had marked the early English and European settlers were reinforced again and again until they became an indelible part of the national heritage. It was on the advancing frontier that the United States found much of its identity as a nation.

2

A New Nation Pushes West, 1776–1815

On October 19, 1781, British general Lord Cornwallis surrendered to revolutionary troops near Yorktown, Virginia. A British marching band played a popular tune that exemplified British feelings on that historic day. The tune they played was "The World Turned Upside Down." The thirteen colonies, a thin strip of populated territory along the eastern shore of North America, had defeated one of the largest empires in the world. The Americans had won their independence.

With the signing of the Treaty of Paris two years later, the new nation's boundaries were roughly identified as 31° north latitude in the South, the Atlantic Ocean in the East, the Great Lakes in the North, and the Mississippi River in the West. Most of this territory remained unsettled. One of the earliest challenges facing the new nation would be to organize this wilderness area as settlers poured across the Appalachian Mountains. How to do this was unclear. What was certain, however, was that Americans would advance the line of settlement as rapidly as they could. And, wherever they settled along the frontier, they helped to forge the American character.

The Advancing Frontier and American Independence

To many Americans, the right to move westward into the continent's interior had been a major reason for fighting the British. Faced with a mounting national debt, created in part by the expenses of colonial administration, the British in 1763 had issued a proclamation forbidding settlement of the Appalachians. Settlers on the edge of the frontier had met with resistance from Native Americans, but the people of England did not wish to shoulder the financial burden necessary to maintain forts manned with British soldiers as protection for these western settlers. The British believed that there was enough unsettled land between the mountains and the Atlantic to satisfy the American settlers. In addition to worrying about the costs of further settlement, the British were also worried about their ability to control their American colonists if the frontier moved beyond the Appalachians.

The British had not counted on the powerful appetite for westward expansion that already characterized the American settlers by the mid-eighteenth century. From the very first, settlers had been pushing colonial civilization westward into the forests of Massachusetts and Maine, the Mohawk Valley in New York, and the Tidewater areas of Virginia and the Carolinas. The political and economic growth of individual colonies had long been influenced by the tensions resulting from the movement westward.

For example, Bacon's Rebellion in Virginia had arisen in the 1670s when western planters under the leadership of Nathaniel Bacon had challenged the colonial government in Jamestown. Bacon and his followers lived on the edge of the advancing frontier in Virginia. They believed that the colony's rulers, living in the settled towns along the Atlantic coast, were unwilling or unable to make laws that applied to frontier conditions. They were especially frustrated by policies that seemed to them to benefit the businesses of the East at the expense of cash-poor settlers along the frontier.

Early experiences like those of Bacon and his followers helped prepare the Americans for their fight for independence. Throughout the 1700s other frontier groups made their presence felt when they challenged the government's tax policies back East. The Paxton Boys of Pennsylvania and the Regulators in the Carolinas were typical of the frontier spirit. Both were frontier groups that took action—at times violent action—against their colonial governments.

In light of such frontier protests some historians have argued that the American Revolution was the culmination of the earliest settlers' struggles on the frontier. These colonists had learned self-reliance from their frontier experiences. They had worked too hard in settling the land to have outsiders impose controls upon them and their profits, no matter whether it was a colonial government or the imperial Proclamation of 1763. The British proclamation failed to stop the advance of the frontier.

When the Revolution began, there were already frontier towns west of the Appalachians. In fact Pittsburgh was well on its way to becoming a major western settlement. As early as the 1760s, people like Daniel Boone had led groups of settlers into the area that would later become Kentucky.

Daniel Boone epitomized the frontiersman. A legend in his own time, he was renowned for pushing the line of civilization ever farther west. His exploits when faced with the dangers of wild animals and angry Indians, became part of the legend of the frontier. Boone's was indeed a remarkable life. As early as 1765 he explored and purchased land near Pensacola, Florida, a wilderness area at that time. When Kentucky began to fill up in the 1780s, he moved his family even farther west, eventually settling west of St. Louis, Missouri, in 1799. In 1814, when he was eighty years old, he explored the region that would later become Yellowstone National Park.

On each frontier visited by Boone life was harsh, and the settlers shared characteristics that would eventually come to be synonymous with America. The settlers of Boone's era made buttons from the bones of animals, wore deerskin clothing, used wooden dishes, and crafted their furniture without benefit of the iron nails that were left far behind in the iron factories of the East. Their habits were primitive by necessity and not dissimilar from those of their ancestors on earlier frontiers. In Kentucky Boone and his people were threatened by wild animals, physical hardship, economic ruin, and occasionally defensive Indians who rightly feared that the white settlers' advancing frontier would mean the end of their way of life.

All of these experiences were similar to those of settlers along earlier frontiers. For example, the records for Hadley, Massachusetts, a town in the western part of the state, relate the following treatment for a hostile Indian in the 1670s: "This aforesaid Indian was ordered to be tourne to peeces by dogs, and she was so dealt with." At about this same time the people of Hadley begged the General Court (the colony's legislature) not to raise their taxes and to accept goods in place of coin as payment. The shortage of hard cash that would plague the settlers of Kentucky a century later was already part of frontier complaints. A 1675 petition from Hadley read, "Not one in ten of the inhabitants hath any income of money. . . . Let it be enough for us to pay in corn . . ."

Shortage of cash, tax burdens, protection from Indians—all of these were frontier issues. With the coming of the Revolution, they would become American issues as frontier people joined with Easterners in the battle against England.

As soon as the Revolution ended, thousands of people rushed to join the movement west. They did so in order to help tame the wilderness and to have new farmlands and new opportunities for economic gain. People looking toward Boonesborough, Kentucky, and the primitive frontier conditions in that area did not expect to live like Boone and his family for long. By filling up Tennessee, Kentucky, and then the Ohio Valley with settlers, they hoped to bring civilization to the frontier as rapidly as possible, at the same time preserving for themselves financial reward and, usually, large plots of land.

Organizing the Western Lands
Right from the beginning, the government of the new nation faced the problems of organization and settlement of western lands. The ratification of the first form of government—the Articles of Confederation—was delayed while the various colonies wrangled over the disposition of their western lands. In many cases seaboard colonies laid vague claims to territories running all the way west to the Mississippi. The Articles were finally ratified when all the colonies, even mighty Virginia, agreed to turn over their unsettled western land to the central government. Between 1781 and the turn of the nineteenth century, New York, Virginia, Massachusetts, Connecticut, the Carolinas, and Georgia turned over nearly 250 million acres to the federal government.

Faced by huge war debts, the Confederation Congress, the legislative body responsible for running the new nation, saw in the western lands a ready source of revenue to help pay for the war. Unfortunately, the plans for federal land sales flew in the face of another idea, highly cherished by many citizens of the new nation. This was the idea that all unsettled land should be free for the taking. Many colonists, particularly those along the advancing frontier, believed that they had fought the Revolutionary War in order to free the land from government control. In England the laws favored primogeniture, the principle that all property should be handed from father to oldest son. Westerners believed this system was wrong and un-American, particularly on a continent where unsettled land seemed to stretch forever. They believed that western lands should be open to claim on a first-come-first-served basis to any settlers who improved the land. Legally this idea was known as the right of preemption. Thomas Jefferson supported preemption. He championed westward expansion by the people he called yeoman farmers. These were the small settlers who he believed formed the backbone of the nation and its economy. He did not want their hard-earned dollars to go to the federal government in land sales. Arguing against such federal land sales, he said, "They [small farmers] will settle the land in spite of everybody."

Many congressmen agreed with Jefferson in part. They recognized that the United States was an agricultural nation. Farmers valued land as the single most important economic element. To further the agricultural development of the nation, the Congress decided to sell the lands north of the Ohio River in the area known as the Old Northwest Territory. The law providing for this sale was titled the Land Ordinance of 1785.

The Land Ordinance of 1785 was designed to make money for the federal government. In 1784 Thomas Jefferson had proposed to Congress that the rich agricultural land of the Ohio frontier be organized into 10 districts bearing such romantic classical names as Polypotamia, Metropotamia, and Sylvania. The Land Ordinance of 1785 provided for the establishment of townships rather than districts. Each of the townships would be comprised of 36 sections, each section 1 square mile in area (about 640 acres). Squatters who were already farming in the new areas could purchase the 640-acre sections by going to land auctions back East. In a time of crude transportation and cash shortages in the Ohio Valley, most squatters preferred to stay on "their" land and take their chances. After all, they had the right of preemption on their side.

Land companies stimulated settlement. When land was actually purchased at auction, the buyer was most likely to be a land company that sold the land at a higher price to settlers. This was known as speculation. Speculators may not have been the buyers Congress had in mind, but they continued to proliferate until the end of the eighteenth century. By placing moneymaking near the top of its list of priorities for western development, Congress insured the dominance of the speculators in land purchases.

There were many drawbacks in terms of fraud and corruption, but speculation had a real place in a free enterprise system. In 1787 the Ohio Company founded Marietta on the Muskingum River. Nearly one million acres of land passed to Revolutionary War veterans through the speculation of the Ohio Company. The Connecticut Land Company settled Cleveland in 1795, and by 1800 the settlement boasted 1,300 people. The area was called the "Western Reserve," because Connecticut had reserved it when it surrendered claim to all other western lands in 1786. (The name of the company is preserved today at Case Western Reserve University in Cleveland). Another important result of land speculation was the founding of the city of Buffalo in 1799. This village on the Niagara frontier, founded by the Holland Land Company, was destined to become the "gateway to the midwest," a land port through which thousands of settlers would pass.

The land companies did more than stimulate pioneers to move west. In the words of western historian Ray A. Billington in *The Westward Movement in the United States,* "The companies cleared streams and harbors, built roads, erected grist and saw mills, laid out model farms, founded villages and even provided taverns, theatres, and race tracks." The land companies can be credited with helping civilization progress into the wilderness, not only in the Northwest, but elsewhere. Wherever the frontier advanced, speculation moved with it.

The first settlers in Ohio came from Connecticut, making the journey of six hundred miles in around ninety days.

The central government may not have earned as much money as it might have wished during the land sales of the mid-1780s, but a secondary goal was quickly realized. The Ohio Valley filled with Americans. As these settlers poured into the new territory, it became clear that the central government of the United States needed to establish some form of government for the new territory. Most people assumed that these new regions would become part of the new nation, but not everyone agreed. There were sporadic attempts to set up separate republics and separate kingdoms in the frontier areas.

Communication with and transportation to the original area of colonization was difficult and hazardous. People argued that a land area as spread out as the Ohio Valley could never be effectively connected to the federal capital back East. As settlement moved closer to the Spanish possessions along the Mississippi River, it was even argued by some that frontier allegiance belonged to the Spanish king rather than to the American Congress.

Congress also faced the problem of territorial government and, in one of the greatest acts of its short existence, passed the Land Ordinance of 1787, which came to be known as the Northwest Ordinance. This document was designed to incorporate areas of frontier settlement into the new nation. Although originally intended to apply only to the Old Northwest Territory, the Ordinance of 1787 proved so effective that the principles it contained were used successfully for the next 150 years. The Ordinance outlined three steps that each new area of settlement would take on the way to becoming a full-fledged state.

When settlers began to move into an area, the region was organized as a territory with a governor, a secretary, and three judges. As soon as the population numbered five thousand adult white males, a territorial legislature was to be elected. Finally, when the population reached sixty thousand white males, a constitutional convention was called, and the territory could apply for statehood. In the Old Northwest Territory the new constitution had to provide for a bill of rights, free public education, and the abolition of slavery. Once the state was admitted to the Union, its citizens gained representation in Congress on an absolutely equal basis with the older states. For white males, at least, the Ordinance of 1787 promised democracy and equal economic opportunity.

It is important for understanding the history of the nation, as well as the history of the movement west, to recognize the significance of the congressional decision that new territories would become states, equal politically to the original thirteen. The Congress could have voted to give western lands a secondary, colonial status. Had it done so, the West as a political force would have played a much different role and would have undoubtedly experienced a much slower economic development.

Ongoing Problems:
The British and the Indians
The end of the war and the establishment of a process for achieving statehood stimulated the settlement of the West. In addition, two treaties in the 1790s helped clear the path to settlement. In spite of the American victory in the Revolution, British troops remained in forts in the Ohio Valley. For many years the Americans had to tolerate this British presence because they had neither the troops nor the money to finance a military campaign to remove them. These troops became an issue

between the earliest political parties, the Federalists (followers of John Adams) and the Democratic-Republicans (followers of Thomas Jefferson).

The Federalists wanted to reestablish friendly relations with Great Britain as rapidly as possible and were eager to settle the issue of the British troops diplomatically. Jefferson's followers, on the other hand, favored relations with France over relations with Great Britain. They saw the English troops as an insult to American honor. After all, they argued, the British should have evacuated the northwestern forts under the 1783 Treaty of Paris. For example, Fort Miami in the Maumee River Valley clearly lay within the American boundaries. Yet British troops remained stationed at this fort and were accused of stirring up Indian attacks against nearby American settlements.

In November of 1794, the British and Americans signed a treaty which provided for the removal of British troops from the Old Northwest Territory. Named the Jay Treaty after its negotiator, John Jay, the treaty came under heavy criticism from the followers of Thomas Jefferson. They believed that Jay and John Adams had not been tough enough with the British. In return for the British surrender of the forts, the Americans agreed to admit British ships into American harbors on terms that were very favorable to the British. The American government also agreed to pay pre-Revolutionary debts owed to British creditors. It seemed that John Jay had given up too much.

The settlers did not care about what had been given up in the treaty. They were just glad that the British were finally gone. However, an even greater threat remained—Indians. Native Americans who did not share the culture and ideas of the white settlers proved to be significant impediments to settlement. Although there were many instances of cooperation between the two groups, too often the Indians' right to the land was disregarded by the white settlers. Frustrated by the settlement of their hunting grounds, the Indians retaliated by burning settlers' cabins and murdering the inhabitants.

The settlers were destined to win, however, as the frontier advanced inexorably. Under the Treaty of Greenville the lands in the Ohio Valley were signed over to white settlers by the Indian tribes in that area. Negotiated by William H. Harrison, an army officer and Indian fighter with political ambition, the Treaty of Greenville marked the first major cheating of the Indians by the future president of the United States. Most western settlers agreed with Harrison's analysis that the Indians were "wretched savages." Even those like Thomas Jefferson who did not share Harrison's sentiments believed that the Ohio lands' rightful owners were white farmers. As the settlers poured into the Ohio Valley, they pushed the Indians farther west, a process that had begun along the Atlantic coast in the early 1600s and would continue until the conquest of the Plains Indians at the end of the nineteenth century. With each forced move to a new region, the Indians lost population.

With the gradual removal of the Indian threat east of the Mississippi, new states rapidly entered the Union. By the time George Washington left office in 1797, Kentucky and Tennessee had become the fifteenth and sixteenth states (Vermont had been the fourteenth). Within new states, as Robert Riegel has written, "the culture of a particular section of the East was reproduced time after time under new conditions." For the most part Virginians and Carolinians filled Kentucky and Tennessee, Pennsylvanians moved into Ohio, and

This artist's interpretation of the signing of the Treaty of Greenville suggests that the Indians willingly surrendered their lands in the Ohio Valley to white farmers.

New Englanders moved through Western New York to the Great Lakes.

*New Territory and
a New War with England*
Progress was measured in terms of population growth because increased population insured statehood. Ohio became the seventeenth state in 1803 and by the outbreak of the War of 1812 boasted a population of 250,000. The citizens of the Indiana Territory elected their first legislature in 1805 and Illinois did the same in 1812. Meanwhile, an entirely new area had been opened for settlement. This was the Old Southwest.

In 1795 Spain and the United States signed Pinckney's Treaty (officially, the Treaty of San Lorenzo). Among other things this treaty provided that the Mississippi River would be open to American navigation and that American ships would have the right to deposit cargoes at the port of New Orleans without paying duty. These peaceful negotiations stimulated migration to the Southwest Territory—future states of Alabama and Mississippi—which had been originally organized under that name in 1790. By 1800, 300,000 settlers lived in this region, and their numbers increased rapidly over the next decade.

The invention of the cotton gin in 1793 had insured the profitability of the plantation system in raising cotton. Because the gin provided an efficient way to remove the seeds, cotton became a major cash crop that could be grown economically on huge plantations, with many slaves to plant, hoe, and harvest the bolls. Small farmers could not compete in this kind of cash-crop economy. Large plantation and slave labor combined to push the small white farmers onto the poorer land. Because cotton production exhausted lands quickly, the plantations expanded into the southwest. The Southwest Territory filled rapidly with cotton growers.

Migration into both the Old Northwest and the Southwest Territory halted almost completely with the outbreak of the War of 1812. Ironically, Westerners were among the most vocal supporters of this war. Young congressional representatives hailing from the new western states were called "War Hawks" because they favored the war. The Ohio Valley had been suffering from an economic depression for several years immediately preceding the outbreak of the war. Many western politicians blamed the British for this economic plight. England controlled the seas, they reasoned, so England must be responsible for the trade problems that they believed underlay the depression. In addition to blaming England for their economic woes, the western War Hawks believed that the British supported the continuing Indian warfare in the Old Northwest. A successful war with England would end Indian hostilities by removing the British instigators from the territory. Finally, the War Hawks wanted more land. Specifically, they hoped to win Canada from Great Britain.

The War of 1812 accomplished none of the West's immediate goals. The flow of emigrants stopped during the war, and the economic situation worsened, at least for the duration. When the war ended, no territory had changed hands. The most misguided of the Western claims had been their espousal of war as a way to end Native American hostility. Not England, but William H. Harrison, should have been held accountable for Indian attacks on pioneer settlements. The unfairness of the Treaty of Greenville contributed far more to Indian hostility than had the instigation of the British.

The British had not had to encourage the Indians

to make war on the settlers. Harrison's greed for new land and lack of respect for the Indians had pushed the Indians to unite under the leadership of Tecumseh, an Indian chieftain. This Shawnee warrior, along with his brother, The Prophet, offered strength and hope to the Indians.

Harrison, first as a military commander and then as a territorial governor, had repeatedly abused and cheated the Indians. His technique was to bribe a fragment of a tribe or a few chieftains into signing treaties involving lands well beyond their jurisdiction. For example, in 1809 he managed to persuade two small tribes to sell over three million acres of land at approximately one-half cent per acre. (The federal government was selling similar land to its citizens at the "bargain" price of two dollars per acre.) In 1810 when Tecumseh said of the white Americans, "They have driven us from the great salt water, [and] forced us over the mountains . . . ," he knew precisely who his enemies were. Tecumseh and his followers carried on the western theatre of the war until their leader's death in 1813. Even Harrison was forced to admit that Tecumseh was "one of those . . . geniuses [who] spring up occasionally to produce revolutions."

Harrison was not the only future president who made his reputation fighting Indians during these years. General Andrew Jackson, the hero of New Orleans, also battled the Indians during the War of 1812. Jackson is reputedly the author of the quotation, "The only good Indian is a dead Indian." Whether he said this or not, he acted as though he believed it. As he and his troops moved through the Southwest, Jackson wantonly destroyed Indian property and took Indian lives. The tribes he encountered were called "The Five Civilized Tribes." Of all the eastern tribes, they had done the most to accommodate to the ways of the white settlers. For this reason their slaughter by Jackson was even more shocking.

When the War of 1812 ended, the Indian threat east of the Mississippi had been removed. Ray Billington has compared the nation at the end of this war to a "giant triangle . . . with its base along the Atlantic seaboard and its apex at the junction of the Ohio and Mississippi rivers." North and south of this triangle were the lands that would be settled in the next wave of migration.

The Louisiana Purchase
If Billington's triangle roughly represented the area of land settled by 1815, it did not begin to take into account all the territory owned by the United States at that point. In 1803 President Thomas Jefferson had authorized the purchase of a vast amount of land that Napoleon Bonaparte wished to sell. Bonaparte had acquired this land from Spain in the course of his European conquests. In 1803 he was far more interested in financing his battle with England than he was in expanding his empire to the North American continent. In fact Napoleon had never seen the land that made up the Louisiana Purchase. Sight unseen he sold 523,446,400 acres of land to the United States for $15 million, or roughly 4¢ an acre. By this one purchase, Jefferson doubled the size of the nation and acquired New Orleans and all or part of what would become the states of Louisiana, Arkansas, Missouri, Iowa, the Dakotas, Nebraska, Kansas, Oklahoma, Colorado, Wyoming, and Montana.

Jefferson's purchase was controversial. He himself had long maintained that neither Congress nor the president should do anything that was not specifically allowed by the Constitution. Nowhere did the Constitution authorize the president to purchase additional land for the nation's expansion. Yet Jefferson felt that the purchase was right and expansion was inevitable. Like many nineteenth-century Americans he believed that the country's wealth and progress depended upon the continual expansion of its agriculture. Agriculture depended upon land. Furthermore, Jefferson was an amateur natural scientist. He was well aware of the rich diversity of the flora and fauna in the wilderness of his native state, Virginia, and he wanted to learn about all the natural phenomena that the uncharted Louisiana Purchase might hold.

Almost before the ink dried on the purchase agreement, Jefferson commissioned two men to lead an expedition to explore the new territory. William Clark and Meriwether Lewis led the first expedition overland across the continental United States. Although their purpose was to explore and not to settle, it was clear from their expedition that the nation could expand west into the new territory. They found plentiful game, navigable rivers, and good soil.

Before the settlers came, however, the new area was explored by American traders. Individual French fur traders had made early forays into the Mississippi wilderness, but after the Louisiana Purchase American fur traders were more numerous and well publicized. Kit Carson and Jim Bridger were perhaps the most famous members of this unique wilderness fraternity. They resembled Daniel Boone in that they could live comfortably with the wilderness and were able to overcome the most hazardous natural obstacles. Bridger was the senior of the two. A native Virginian, he followed the expansion of the country, moving to Missouri with his parents and then striking out on his own as a trapper.

Jim Bridger earned a reputation as a storyteller because he regaled his listeners with tales of the phenomena now located in Yellowstone Park. A geyser that shot up regularly and on schedule ("Old Faithful") was a typically unbelievable subject of his tales. Nature that acted larger than life was the stock in trade of the woodsman's stories and became a part of the frontier heritage. The more startling the act of nature, the greater the reputation of the people who conquered it.

Kit Carson's legend was greater than Bridger's, but made of the same frontier lore. Born in Kentucky in 1809, Carson had crossed the country to California by 1829. He spent most of the decades of the 1830s and 1840s trapping and trading in Idaho. Although Carson was illiterate, he dictated his adventures to an army surgeon who embellished Carson's story. By the 1860s the stories of Kit Carson's adventures had become stock schoolboy reading. In them Carson fought wild animals, savage Indians, and natural disasters. He was invariably the winner through courage, cunning, and coolness under pressure. He was, after all, a Westerner and a frontiersman, in short, a true American.

The years that the fur traders dominated the wilderness were short-lived as settlers moved quickly into the new territory. Nevertheless, their importance lay in their being the first white Americans in the region. In most cases they easily made the transition from trapping to guiding parties of settlers. Fur traders, because of the solitary nature of their work, helped to create the romantic western ideal of the individual who battled nature. In reality fur traders were all sorts of people. One of the most successful was a Harvard-educated poet, Albert Pike. Yet another was Charles Gardner, a desperate character who had been forced to leave Philadelphia when he allegedly set a convent on

BEADLE'S DIME NEW YORK LIBRARY

COPYRIGHTED IN 1878, BY BEADLE & ADAMS.

Vol. I. Complete In One Number. Beadle & Adams, Publishers, No. 98 William Street, New York. Price Ten Cents. No. 3.

Kit Carson, Jr., the Crack Shot of the West.

A WILD LIFE ROMANCE, BY "BUCKSKIN SAM."

fire. Occasionally black men, eager to flee the racial injustice of eastern society, headed west as fur traders.

The solitary life of the fur trappers would be short-lived. When the War of 1812 ended in 1815, there were eighteen states in the Union, and in the nation's consciousness America's western boundary no longer stopped at the Mississippi. With the end of the war came the next great push west. In the last full year of the war, 1814, one million acres of western land were sold, and by 1818 this number was tripling annually. The "Great Migration" had begun.

The way of life of the fur trader or the settler on the advancing frontier was fast becoming synonymous with the American way of life. The frontier was an important influence on the way other people thought about Americans and the way Americans thought about themselves. Wherever there was wilderness, people moved to conquer it. In cutting down the forests, fighting the Indians, and populating the new land, Americans demonstrated courage, energy, and optimism. These were the positive traits associated with the frontier. At the same time people along the advancing frontier were also characterized by materialism, greed, and racism.

This "dime novel" tells the story of the legendary trapper and frontiersman Kit Carson.

3   Manifest Destiny: Americans Fill the Continent

With the end of the War of 1812, great migration of Americans to the West began. Prosperity returned to the country, and prosperity meant that more families could afford the trek west. Between 1815 and 1850 thirteen new states came into the Union, all populated by people who had headed west. Whether ruled by a longing for land or for gold, these nineteenth-century Westerners would add to the image and legend of life on the frontier.

Pioneers applauded the changes that had occurred during the War of 1812. As reprehensible as the early 19th century treatment of Indians seems to twentieth century Americans, the exploits of generals Andrew Jackson and William H. Harrison made it safer for white farmers to live along the edge of the frontier. The war had stimulated the economy; money fueled the movement west. And, in the years after the war, technological advances, particularly in the fields of transportation and communication, insured that people on the advancing frontier could maintain contact with people back East. The federal government constructed a National Road leading west across the Appalachians and on to Missouri. Robert Fulton perfected the steamboat, an invention that enabled farmers in the Ohio and Mississippi river valleys to get their produce to market far more easily than they had been able to do in previous years.

Land Sales and Population Boom
By 1820, a mere five years after the conclusion of the war, two and one-quarter million people, one-fourth of

the nation's population, lived in western territories. As many people lived west of the Appalachians by 1820 as had lived in the original thirteen states at the time of independence. Ohio remained the most heavily populated area west of the mountains, but Kentucky was almost as well populated as Ohio, and Tennessee and Louisiana were not far behind. Southerners were pushing into Mississippi and Alabama as cotton expanded west of Georgia.

For families on the western fringes of civilization, the pattern of settlement had not changed much since the days of Daniel Boone. Although federal land sales accounted for much of the new property that was settled, settlers still moved ahead of the government. To avoid the problems of conflicting claims and rampant speculation that had plagued land sales since the Revolution, the federal government had established a new department to regulate land sales. In 1812 the General Land Office was formed under the supervision of the Treasury Department (in 1849 it was moved to the Department of Interior).

In spite of this formal organization of land sales, government surveyors could not keep ahead of the flood of migrants. Inexpensive as the land was, some people could not afford it. Some who could afford it believed that the presence of limitless land along the frontier meant that any person should have free access to a homestead. Such people "squatted" on federal lands; they settled without buying the property or filing proper claims. These "squatters" hoped that by the time the surveyors reached them, they would either be able to afford the purchase price or would be exempt from paying because of the improvements they had made to the land.

By today's standards, western property seems cheap.

On the average, land sold for roughly $2 an acre. However, frontier areas were far removed from banks that could provide loans. Hard money—coins and bank bills—was scarce on the frontier, where people were most likely to trade by barter. Under the terms of the Land Acts of 1800 and 1804, early western emigrants had had to purchase a minimum of 320 acres of land at $2 per acre. The purchase price of $640 was a large sum, and settlers had to put down one quarter of the money in cash.

By 1820 many Westerners were plagued by debt. Settlers owed over $20 million on this land, money they could not pay. The government recognized this problem. By the terms of the Land Act of 1820, lots of 80 acres could be sold. Government officials figured that if settlers were able to buy smaller pieces of land, they would be better able to afford their purchases. In addition, the Land Act of 1820 dropped the price per acre by 75¢. At the same time, however, credit for land purchases was disallowed. Although the land was cheaper, the settlers had to pay the full price in cash. It was hoped that more settlers would be able to afford to buy land and that the government would not be faced with so many bad debts after the settlers reached the West. In spite of debt and credit problems, land sales increased throughout the 1820s and 1830s at such a rapid rate that a new saying came into the American language. "Doing a land-office business" meant enjoying booming success in sales.

Certainly there was a population boom. Between 1820 and 1840 the population of Ohio grew three times, the population of Indiana grew four times, and the population of Illinois grew eight times. In the census reports for 1820, 1830, and 1840 Ohio, Kentucky, and Tennessee were all listed among the ten most populous states—and these had been largely areas of uncharted wilderness as recently as 1800. Indiana made the list in 1840. In general the population of the West during those years grew twice as rapidly as that of the United States. Of the twenty-six states in the Union by 1840, eleven were located west of the mountains.

Although the greatest numbers of Easterners migrated to northwestern areas, the Southwest frontier experienced a major population boom during these same years. The Louisiana Purchase had insured that the port of New Orleans would be available for southwestern farmers to ship their cotton and other products. Because of New Orleans' importance as a harbor and the years of Spanish and French settlement there, Louisiana already had a large population. That territory became a state in 1812. The new postwar migration filled in the states between Louisiana and the coast. By 1817 Mississippi had gained statehood. Alabama followed in 1819 and Missouri in 1821.

The Southwestern Frontier
Statehood for Mississippi and Alabama highlighted the movement into the Southwest Territory. The soil in this region—an area that would come to be known as the "Deep South"—was among the richest in the nation, and its fertility proved excellent for cotton production. Along the Southwest frontier, conditions were very similar to those in the Northwest. Life was primitive, and communication and transportation systems were very weak in the early years of settlement.

In one very important way, however, the advancing southwestern frontier differed significantly from the frontier in the Northwest. Here Turner's theory seems to break down. He argued that democracy was forged along the frontier. However, the "Alabama Fever" that drove settlers into the Southwest brought with it a long-lasting sickness that was the opposite of democracy. Many of the settlers on the southwest frontier were plantation owners, people who wanted to make their fortunes by expanding cotton cultivation. Along with cotton went the institution of slavery. The hallmarks of democracy that characterized the Northwest frontier—equal opportunity, political democracy, and social mobility—seemed not to predominate in the South. Here existed rigid class distinctions, aristocratic political rule, and a feudal labor system. True, self-reliance, personal strength and upward mobility were prized qualities, but only for the white males in the society.

Cities Grow Along the Frontier
One other trait distinguished the northern frontier from the southern frontier. In the North the increasing population was accompanied by rapid urbanization along frontier areas. Cities sprang up in the west as fast as enterprising pioneers could build them. Settlers who struggled on the edge of the wilderness saw the coming of banks, mills, and general stores as marks of progress and signs that they had met their goal of taming the wild territory.

By the 1830s it was fair to say that the settlements along the Ohio River could no longer be called frontier areas. By 1840 Cincinnati had earned the nickname "Queen City of the West" and was the sixth largest American city. Buffalo was growing rapidly and served as a jumping-off place for settlers moving west. Here on the Niagara frontier farmers could stock their wagons before heading off to new lands in the wilderness. Throughout the 1830s an average of seventy-five thousand people passed through Buffalo each year on their way to new farms and new fortunes.

Cincinnati, Ohio, the "Queen City of the West," as it appeared in 1848

The new cities of the West were unique blends of pioneer rawness and imitation of the culture left behind. In many areas, sanitation and health conditions were poor. Nevertheless, as quickly as possible the settlers built schools and even colleges and universities. Transylvania University in Lexington, Kentucky, was the first institution of higher learning west of the Appalachians, but it was followed in short succession by a host of others in Ohio, Tennessee, and Indiana.

The presence of a local newspaper was a sure sign that a settlement was on its way to urbanization. Newspapers were vitally important in areas removed from easy communication with the East. Newspaper presses were often the first "luxury" items hauled through the wilderness to the new towns along the frontier. Pittsburgh had claimed the first journal west of the Appalachians as early as 1786. These early newspapers served to link widespread homesteads. The editor frequently used the paper as a way to publicize the progress of the town and attract new money to the area.

"Manifest Destiny" and Texas
Not surprisingly, it was a newspaper editor who coined the phrase that would forever be linked with westward expansion in the American mind. In 1845 John L. O'Sullivan, a newspaperman in New York City, wrote that it was the "manifest destiny" of Americans to fill in the entire continent. Those sentiments were echoed by an energetic young western congressman, Stephen Douglas of Illinois, who proclaimed on the floor of Congress that the United States should stretch from the Atlantic to the Pacific Ocean. Douglas called these bodies of water "those boundaries which the god of nature had marked out." From the 1840s on, people believed

with Douglas that it was America's natural or divine right to stretch from "sea to shining sea."

Much of the impetus for O'Sullivan's writing stemmed from his belief that the United States should expand into Texas. As early as 1821 American settlers had moved into Texas, an area that had long been a part of Mexico. When Moses Austin and his son Stephen first sought to purchase land from Mexico for themselves and their followers, the Mexicans were delighted. They sold thousands of acres of land to the Austins and others for pennies an acre.

By 1830 there were thousands of Americans living in Texas. This seemed like enough to the Mexicans. They forbad any more American settlement after this year. Not only were they worried about the large number of Americans moving into their country, they were also concerned about the anti-Catholic and proslavery sentiments that these settlers from the white South brought with them.

The Mexicans were predominantly Roman Catholic and Roman Catholicism was their official religion. The predominantly Protestant Americans did not wish to support the Catholic Church. In fact, they ridiculed it and fought against paying Mexican taxes that supported this established religion. Furthermore, Mexico had outlawed slavery and did not want American Southerners bringing the slavery system into Texas.

The Mexicans were right to worry. Americans living in Texas became more and more reluctant to follow Mexican laws. Like pioneers before them in other areas, they wanted most to re-create the life they had left behind. That life was American, not Mexican. Because the Mexicans were Roman Catholic, it was easy for Protestant Americans to rationalize their "superiority" over their hosts. After all, everything in United States history to that point had seemed to justify white Protestantism as the morally superior, progressive way of life.

In 1836, after a brief war, the inhabitants of Texas declared their independence from Mexico. In an essay on the history of the far western frontier, Harvey L. Carter has explained the Texas Revolution this way, "Regardless of other causes . . . it is best explained as a dynamic manifestation of the moving American frontier. In the resulting clash of . . . Anglo and Hispanic cultures, the latter, which was more static, was forced to give way." Brash Americans, imbued with the belief that they had a divine right to all territory in North America ran roughshod over a Spanish culture that had existed in Mexico for three hundred years.

The long-range goal of the American Texans was to affiliate as a state with the United States, a goal they reached in the mid-1840s, spurred on by the national fever for "Manifest Destiny." In American minds, God and nature clearly intended for Texas to be part of the United States. A similar process for adding new land to the United States would be followed again and again, most clearly in Oregon and California. In those two areas, too, the settlers would move in peacefully, eventually feel both the strength of their numbers and the burden of being ruled by another nation, revolt, and finally attach themselves to the United States.

The Oregon Trail—
Missionaries, Settlers, Politicians
Throughout the 1840s people spoke of "Oregon Fever," a condition afflicting those who believed that the Oregon frontier should be the next logical step in westward expansion. In 1841 a small group of settlers set out bravely from the East on their way to Oregon. After

stocking their wagons in Missouri, they followed the Platte River through South Pass, across the Green River to the Bear River Valley, where the party split into two groups. Half the settlers headed north along the Snake River to the Willamette Valley, while the other half turned south. The second group traveled along the Humboldt River, across the Sierra Nevada Mountains, and into California's San Joaquin Valley.

The northern route became the famous Oregon Trail. Even before these settlers made the trek along the Oregon Trail, the area attracted Protestant missionaries, drawn to the area by the opportunity to Christianize the "heathen" Indians living there. Methodists and Presbyterians flocked west to engage in this kind of activity. Since the first Thanksgiving feast along the Massachusetts coast, white Protestants had believed it to be their duty to Christianize all peoples who held beliefs different from theirs. The Indians had always been prime subjects for this missionizing. Then in 1831 four western Indians allegedly appeared in St. Louis, Missouri, asking for a Bible so that they could learn the Christian faith. Whether or not the Indians were representative, their visit to St. Louis was widely publicized as proof that western Indians yearned for Christian teaching. The migration of the missionaries began.

First west was Rev. Jason Lee, a Methodist minister who headed for Oregon in 1834. He was quickly followed by Marcus Whitman and Henry Spalding, Presbyterian ministers. Whitman and Spalding were accompanied by their wives, Narcissa and Eliza. These two women were among the first white women to make the overland trek. Their example proved that families could migrate West, and the rush was on. By the mid-1840s, five thousand people lived in Oregon. Enthusiasm for Oregon was dampened briefly in 1847 when the Whitmans and others were killed by Cayuse Indians, but it was generally believed to be only a matter of time before the Indians were subdued and Oregon made a state.

As with Texas, however, Oregon's development as a state involved wresting control of the area from another nation. In this case the other nation was Great Britain. The British claimed the Oregon Territory as part of Canada, and there were some British settlers and British officials in the area. Ownership of Oregon became a topic in the presidential campaign of 1844. The Democratic candidate, James Polk, was a firm believer in expansion. He stood for election on a platform that included the annexation of Texas. Annexation would mean adding that region to the United States. In addition, Polk argued that Oregon naturally belonged to the United States. In fact, his best-remembered campaign slogan was coined around the issue of the possession of Oregon. "Fifty-four forty or fight!" yelled Polk's supporters. By this phrase they meant that the northern border of the United States in the area of Oregon should extend to the latitude 54° 40'. If Britain were not prepared to recognize this claim, Polk's supporters urged that the United States go to war to settle the conflict.

Once in office Polk's enthusiasm for a war with Great Britain cooled. In 1846 his secretary of state, James Buchanan, negotiated a treaty with Great Britain that settled the Oregon controversy. The United States did not gain territory as far north as the fifty-fourth parallel. Instead the forty-ninth parallel, which served as the boundary with Canada from the Great Lakes to Montana, was extended to the Pacific Ocean. The treaty was negotiated amiably and paved the way for further settlement and the eventual statehood of Oregon.

Death and Hardship Along the Trail
The political hurdle to the settlement of Oregon was only one of the obstacles Easterners had to overcome in making the trek west in the 1840s. The average American farmer planning to settle in the West probably felt confident that his farm would be protected by the flag of the United States eventually. What was of far more immediate concern to these pioneers was whether or not they and their families would survive the dangerous journey west.

In 1841 John Bidwell proved that the trip could be made when he led the first true family group along the Oregon Trail. With him traveled the first large numbers of pioneer women and children to make the trip across the Rocky Mountains. The Bidwell group has been called "the advance guard of the irresistible march of the American people westward." Bidwell, and all the other settlers who made the arduous journey in the 1840s, believed they were leaving civilization for only a short period of time. They believed that thousands of emigrants from the East would follow them and that they could re-create the civilization of the East in the new lands out West. Wrote one Peter Burnett in 1845 at the time of his migration west, "I saw that a great American community would grow up, in the space of a few years, upon the shores of the distant Pacific."

Burnett and Bidwell counted on the pioneer spirit of the American people to propel settlers west. To make the journey called for a sense of adventure, optimism, strength, courage, money, and luck. The people making this journey were not impoverished. The trip was long, and unexpected expenses could force a family to turn back penniless or to stop before it reached its goal. As James Hewitt describes in *Eye-Witness to Wagon Trains West*, "a family needed at least one covered wagon, three yoke of oxen to pull it, and provisions to last five to six months' arduous travel."

No matter how carefully a family prepared for the trip west, the hardships were many and often unpredictable. The death rate among children was high, and many small graves dotted the trail, mute testimony to the passing caravans of the threat the wilderness held. Not surprisingly babies born along the trail were often buried along the trail. Those who survived were often given names that testified to their adventures. For example, Helen Independence Miller was born on a trip west in 1844.

Timing was crucial. It was important that the wagon trains leave Missouri early in May if they were to cross the Sierra Nevada mountains before heavy snows fell in November. Good leadership was also important. Most wagon trains elected a trail leader, a person responsible for making decisions about amounts of provisions and routes to follow.

Nature was the travelers' enemy. When rivers were swollen by early spring rains, the wagons had to be emptied onto ferries made of waterproofed wagon beds. Cattle, horses, oxen, and people had to wade or swim. Swollen rivers in the spring gave way to dried-up rivers in the summer. Along the way hostile Indians, poisonous snakes, epidemics, buffalo stampedes, and dwindling food supplies added to the hazards of the journey. By early November mountain blizzards swept across the travelers whose goal was to reach California in December.

Although most people made the trip successfully, the Donner Party, a group that met disaster, has become synonymous with the hazards of the trek west. The timing for this trip was all wrong. In July 1846 the Donner Party set out from Illinois. By the time they reached the Sierra Nevadas, the first blizzards of an early winter had begun. Some members of the party separated from others, another grave error. On the trip west, safety was definitely found in numbers, and the group should have stayed together. By the time the survivors reached California their numbers had dwindled severely. Of the eighty-seven people who started the trip, only forty-seven lived to see their destination.

Before the trip ended, the Donner Party had experienced death and cannibalism. Thirteen-year-old Elizabeth Reed, one of the lucky few survivors, wrote of her experiences to a cousin back East: "We had to kill littel [sic] Cash the dog and eat him. We ate his entrails & feet & hide & everything about him. There was 15 in the cabin we was in. . . . There was 10 starved to death. 3 died & the rest ate them."

Fortunately, the experience of the Donner Party was the exception rather than the rule. For every settler who died, hundreds more completed the trip successfully, and they wrote back encouragingly to their friends in the East. Among the most persuasive were the adventurers John Charles Frémont and his ambitious, talented wife, Jessie Benton. Both wrote romantic accounts of their travels west to California with the famous guide Kit Carson. Even little Elizabeth Reed did not discourage her cousin from making the trip west. She advised matter-of-factly, "Never take no cut-off, and hurry along as fast as you can."

California and Gold
The Indian raids that killed the Whitmans may have temporarily discouraged settlers from moving to Oregon, but people continued to move to other areas along the western coast. They looked to the southern or California Trail as the path to new homes and new for-

tunes. In the mid-1840s California was predominantly Mexican and Indian. Although some Americans were recorded as living in California as early as 1816, a census in 1846 found only seven hundred Americans in the area compared with seven thousand Mexicans and ten thousand Indians. In 1850 California entered the Union as the thirty-first state. In the intervening five years, the United States had fought and won a war against Mexico that increased American land holdings by over 330 million acres, including all of present-day California. Happily for American fortunes when gold was discovered in California, the area belonged to the United States, not to Mexico.

Like Texas, California became part of the United States through the aggressive expansionist policy of the early nineteenth century. During James Polk's administration the United States became involved in a border dispute with Mexico. Texas had finally been annexed by the United States in 1845, but Texans and Mexicans disagreed about whether the Rio Grande or the Nueces River should serve as the dividing line between Texas and its former owner, now new neighbor, Mexico. Polk ordered American troops onto the edge of the disputed territory. Mexican forces formed along the southern bank of the Rio Grande. Then, in an act of war, Polk ordered American troops into the disputed territory. Mexican troops fought back, but the outcome was certain from the beginning. The Mexicans had fewer troops, outdated equipment, and little appetite for the conflict. The Americans were victorious.

At the conclusion of the hostilities, the Mexicans and Americans negotiated the Treaty of Guadalupe Hidalgo. Signed in 1848 this treaty transferred to the United States almost all the land that comprises the states of California, New Mexico, Nevada, and Utah, and parts of New Mexico, Colorado, and Wyoming. In return the Mexican government received fifteen million dollars from the United States. In the four short years between 1845 and 1849 the United States had acquired 40 percent of the land that would eventually constitute the forty-eight continental states.

Only the relatively tiny Gadsden Purchase of 1854 remained to complete the map as it looks today. This strip of land, approximately thirty thousand square miles in size, was the subject of yet another boundary dispute between the United States and Mexico. James Gadsden, United States minister to Mexico, offered the Mexicans ten million dollars for the parcel of land that is now included in the southern tips of Arizona and New Mexico. Although the Mexicans resisted the sale, they had no intention of fighting another war with the United States, and the forced sale was concluded in 1853.

Meanwhile a new fever had struck the United States—"gold fever." Ten days before the signing of the Treaty of Guadalupe Hidalgo, gold was discovered by James Marshall at Sutter's Mill on the American River. In 1849 the territorial governor of California, Richard B. Mason, wrote to the War Department, "There is more gold in the country drained by the Sacramento and San Joaquin rivers than would pay the cost of the late war with Mexico a hundred times over." The California gold rush was on.

By mule, by ship, on foot, by oxen, by horse, people poured west into California to make their fortunes in gold. The gold rush was a great adventure that captured the imagination of all Americans because it held all the elements of frontier adventure—rugged living, new wealth, democracy based on ability, optimism, and individual enterprise. The most popular tune of 1849 was "O! Susanna." Its carefree miners' lyrics went like this:

> I'll scrape the mountains clean, old girl
> I'll drain the rivers dry.
> I'm off to California, Susannah, don't you cry.

By the time the gold rush ended, California was a state with a population of 250,000 people, San Francisco had grown into a leading American city, and over $200 million of gold had been mined. Prospectors then turned to the silver fields of Nevada.

Without the discovery of gold, California would undoubtedly still have filled with people. The discovery of gold there and silver in Nevada merely sped up the process. In the twenty years after Bidwell's expedition, more than 350,000 settlers moved west of the Rockies, before the Civil War brought a temporary halt to westward expansion.

4 Manifest Destiny, Politics, and Civil War

When California applied to enter the Union, the western states became the focus of politics. The question of California's statehood became the burning political issue of 1850. The West had been a political factor for years. Between 1850 and 1860, however, it would become an issue in the most monumental struggle the nation had ever faced, a division between North and South that would culminate in civil war.

Jacksonian Democracy and the Frontier
Certainly the advancing frontier had influenced politics before. As early as the 1600s, areas on the edge of the frontier had pushed for Indian protection, land reform, and more liberal voting rights. By so doing, these regions had influenced politics in eastern state capitals. The War of 1812 had been fought in part because of the ambitions of western politicians. In terms of national politics, the frontier assumed a position of central importance in the years after 1820. And in the late 1820s and 1830s a force called Jacksonian democracy revolutionized American political parties. Named for Andrew Jackson, soldier, Indian fighter, territorial governor, and President of the United States (1829–37), Jacksonian democracy shared many characteristics of the man after whom it was named. Both were frontier phenomena.

Andrew Jackson was born before the American Revolution along the frontier in the western Carolinas. (In fact surveys of the area were so primitive that both North and South Carolina claim him as a native son.) The Waxhaw district of the Carolinas was a rough frontier area when Jackson was born, affording no opportunity for culture or education. The opportunity it did provide—as was true in most frontier areas—was advancement for a young man of courage, strength, and optimism. After teenage adventures fighting the British, Jackson read law in a North Carolina office and by the age of twenty-one, was established as an attorney in the frontier town of Nashville, Tennessee. Tennessee would become the base of his political operations and would be the first state to nominate him for president in 1824.

Meanwhile, the frontier society afforded Jackson many opportunities for making and losing large sums of money. Early Nashville was a wild town with a significant Indian population. Jackson became the town's leading lawyer and involved himself in schemes for developing the trade of the area at the same time that he worked to control the area's Indians, an experience that he would later use as an Indian fighter during the War of 1812. Like other frontier settlers, Jackson wanted progress to come rapidly to his section of the West. In the meantime he fought with the more settled regions to insure that the far-western settlements would not be slighted by legislative decisions regarding taxation, representation, and credit.

Jackson believed that settlers in the western areas of the nation, the common people, were not sharing fully in the prosperity of the nation. From the time that a British Redcoat slashed young Jackson's forehead with a sabre, Jackson equated Great Britain with privilege and elitism, and he fought the influence of these forces in American politics. He thought that Easterners were too much like the British. The frontier, he believed, was the home of the true American. Here men and women were measured by strength and courage, and each person earned his success. Politics, he believed, should reflect these qualities. He wanted no property qualification for white men to vote and hold office (universal manhood suffrage). He wanted politics to be controlled by the people. To do this he supported the idea of political conventions to nominate presidential candidates. Delegates to these conventions could be chosen from among the common people and would be free of the control of eastern bankers and senators.

Whether people agreed with Jackson or disagreed with him—and there were many in both categories—he epitomized the increasing impact of the frontier on politics. To his detractors, he was a violent, unmannered, uneducated backwoods man who represented all that was crude and dangerous about the frontier. To his supporters, he was energetic, confident, progressive, loyal, rugged, and courageous. Because of Jackson's political reforms, more groups than ever before did become involved in politics. In this way Jacksonian democracy lends support to Turner's thesis that political freedom arose more swiftly along the line of the frontier.

The Mexican War and Politics
During Jackson's era, the advancing frontier in politics still rested east of the Mississippi. Until the era of Manifest Destiny, in fact, it can be argued that most frontier political issues were fairly local in nature and involved conflicts between the eastern and western portions of a state.

The eastern line of frontier changed rapidly before the 1840s, with each new change bringing political shifts. Not until the conclusion of the Mexican War did the frontier generally equal the West—the vast territory from the Mississippi to the Pacific. Inevitably and at last this great area had to be incorporated into the Union; in being so incorporated it became an area of intense, divisive political concern between the northern and southern halves of the country east of the Mississippi. No sooner would a compromise be reached than a new conflict concerning the West would arise.

The political tension over the advancing western frontier had begun with the outbreak of the Mexican War. This conflict was viewed by many Northerners as a "slaveholders' conspiracy." The boundary dispute with Mexico, northeastern opponents of the war claimed, was a trumped-up excuse for southern congressmen and President Polk to increase the slavery territories of the United States and expand cotton production westward. In fact, the Nueces River had historically delineated the boundary of Texas, and Polk's claim that the Rio Grande marked the boundary was questionable. Given the presence in Texas of many plantations with their system of slavery, it is easy to see why some Northerners feared that southern plantation owners and politicians would attempt to push slavery from Texas throughout the Southwest to California.

Northern artists and writers who favored the abolition of slavery were among the most vocal opponents of the war. In one of the most famous American acts of civil disobedience, the writer Henry David Thoreau refused to pay his taxes because he did not want any of his money supporting the Mexican War. He believed the war was being fought to extend slavery into the West. For his failure to pay, he spent a night in jail.

Another Northerner, a representative from Illinois, a state that had only recently been considered part of the frontier, spoke out in Congress against the war. Like Thoreau, young Whig congressman Abraham Lin-

General Zachary Taylor, third from left, is shown here at his headquarters near Monterrey, Mexico, during the Mexican War.

coln believed that Polk was conspiring with the plantation owners to spread the institution of slavery into the West. Lincoln attempted to pass what came to be known as the "spot resolution." This was a congressional bill demanding that President Polk demonstrate to Congress the exact spot where the Mexicans had begun the war. The incentive for Lincoln's "spot resolution" was Polk's war message in which he had stated, "Mexico has . . . shed American blood upon the American soil." Congress rejected the resolution, and Abraham Lincoln soon thereafter lost his seat in the House of Representatives.

Massachusetts, home of Thoreau, led the antiwar feeling. Both legislative houses in that state voted overwhelmingly to adopt a set of resolves that condemned the war on the grounds that its primary purpose was the extension of slavery. The document adopted in the spring of 1847 stated clearly that "the present war with Mexico . . . was . . . commenced . . . with the triple object of extending slavery, of strengthening the slave power, and of obtaining the control of the Free States."

In spite of northern opposition, of course, the war was fought and fought successfully. Yet the question of the balance between the slave states and free states, which the war opened, would not be laid to rest until the Civil War settled the issue of states' rights versus federal power. Meanwhile, the presence of numerous new states along the advancing frontier would intensify this controversy and lead to the Civil War. With the Mexican War, the West took center stage in the political arena.

Compromises Tried and Failed
In the aftermath of the war, the problems to come were not apparent. The Treaty of Guadalupe Hidalgo had

greatly enlarged the size of the nation and had certainly completed the country's continental destiny. However, there had been vast territorial acquisitions before, and there had been controversy over slavery before, and the nation had reached compromises. After all, in 1820 a compromise line had been drawn across the Louisiana Purchase, above which slavery would not be tolerated. Surely a similar compromise could be worked out this time.

The lands ceded by Mexico were different, however, and different forces were operating here to prevent any compromise. By 1849, when the treaty was signed, the North and South were more clearly defined in terms of their economies and their ways of life. The arguments opposing and defending the institution of slavery had been sharpened. Moderates in the South were less prominent, and in the North the abolitionists' numbers were increasing. Finally for all intents and purposes the Mexican cession, that land acquired from Mexico during the war, marked the end of territorial expansion. The Pacific had been reached. The nation's destiny had been achieved. Decisions about how this portion of the West was settled and where slavery was to be allowed or disallowed took on new importance. There was now no new territory farther west to hold those pioneers who disagreed with whatever decisions were made.

Added to all this were two new issues—the invention of the railroad and the discovery of gold in California. The invention of the railroad meant the promise of swift transportation across the continent and a revolution in marketing. Adventurers in the North and in the South were quick to realize that the section that first claimed the rail lines to the West would surge ahead in the economic power struggle being waged between the North and South. The discovery of gold in California and the rush of settlers to that area meant that rail development would be swift and that the territories would be populated quickly. With rapid population would come demands for statehood.

This situation gained national attention with the inevitable application by California for statehood. In 1849 the territory applied to President Zachary Taylor to become a state. Taylor hoped that Congress would delay any decision on California until at least one other state applied for admission. Throughout the 1820s and 1830s peace had prevailed as states entered the Union in pairs, one free and one slave each time. Taylor hoped that by waiting, the same thing might occur.

Taylor's wish was not to be. Throughout much of 1849 and 1850 the debate over slavery in the territories had raged in Congress and in the nation's newspapers. The showdown on the West had begun. On both sides the spokesmen were elderly statesmen of great stature who had helped define countless constitutional positions in the early years of the nation. Now in what for many of them would be their final great public appearances, these leaders were challenged by the needs of a new nation that had grown to match their youthful dreams of a country spread from ocean to ocean.

John C. Calhoun, senator from South Carolina, led the group supporting the extension of slavery into the new territories. Calhoun began his debate with Daniel Webster in the course of a congressional discussion of territorial government in general. Calhoun had entered Congress in 1811 as a representative from the slave state of South Carolina. He had joined Henry Clay as one of the young "War Hawks" eager to fight with England. Throughout his long congressional career, Calhoun was an ardent supporter of states' rights. He argued that "the United States is not a union of the people, but a league or compact between sovereign states, any of which has the right to judge when the compact is broken and to pronounce any law to be null and void which violates its conditions."

In line with his position on states' rights, Calhoun argued that the Constitution allowed for the institution of slavery and that no act of Congress could constitutionally bar slavery from a new state because that state would have the right to declare the antislavery law "null and void." To Calhoun slavery was a form of labor legitimately recognized by the Constitution. Slaves were property. According to the Constitution a person could not be deprived of his property without due process of law. If Congress persisted in trying to rid the new territory of slavery, then, Calhoun reasoned, the slave states had the right to break from the Union.

Like Calhoun, Daniel Webster had entered Congress at the time of the War of 1812. A native of New Hampshire, he eventually made Boston his home and represented Massachusetts in the United States Senate from 1830 to 1850. As ardent a New Englander as Calhoun was a Southerner, in the course of his long career Webster frequently found himself on the opposite side of the political fence from the South Carolina senator.

Opponents though they were, Calhoun, speaking for the South and Daniel Webster, speaking for the North, had helped to resolve the issue of slavery time and again in the territories without destroying the Union. In 1850 it was left to Henry Clay, senator from Kentucky, to offer a compromise. Clay's career had paralleled those of Webster and Calhoun. He represented the West just as they represented the North and South. During his years in Congress, Clay had earned the nickname of "The Great Compromiser."

Most Americans believed that any compromise supported by Clay, Webster, and Calhoun would certainly save the nation from violent disruption. Meanwhile, President Zachary Taylor insisted that California be admitted as a free state and threatened to send troops into any southern state that failed to support federal laws.

To satisfy all parties, Clay hammered out a compromise with many provisions. In so doing he had Webster's, but not Calhoun's support. Nearing the end of his life, Calhoun was intransigent on the subject of slavery. Nevertheless, the Compromise of 1850 passed both houses of Congress and helped avert war for another decade. The Compromise of 1850 would be Clay's last great effort. Among other issues, the compromise addressed problems of slavery in the District of Columbia, boundary disputes between Texas and New Mexico, and the problem of fugitive slaves. In each instance the North and South had to give a little in order to gain a little. California entered the Union unpaired, as a free state.

War was avoided by the compromise, but it was clear that the volatile combination of territorial expansion and slavery threatened the existence of the nation. As Frederick Merk has written in his *History of the Westward Movement,* "The crisis of 1850 was the price paid by the nation for overindulgence in territorial expansion." The peace that followed the compromise was short-lived. In a few brief years western settlers would roil the political waters again. Each time the North and South clashed over the West, the possibility of war became more certain and the prospects for peace more remote. The frontier that Turner would characterize as a "safety valve" for eastern tensions and pressures seems instead to have become the focal point at which eastern tensions between North and South would explode.

The Kansas-Nebraska Territory
In 1854 the inevitable explosion took place in the Kansas-Nebraska Territory. To a large extent this area had been bypassed as settlers worked their way west to the rich soil and richer mines of California and Oregon. Earlier in the century the federal government had settled large numbers of Indians in this territory. By treaty these Indians claimed the territory. For white settlers to displace them would mean breaking the treaties. While breaking treaties already had far too many historical precedents, most people were willing to bypass this section of the country and leave it to the Indians.

By 1854, however, white settlers wanted the Kansas-Nebraska Territory opened to their settlement. There were many reasons for this. Thousands of travelers heading west had noted the richness of the farmlands in this area. With the rush for gold diminished by 1854, settlers questioned the wisdom of the trek across the Rockies. Farmers looking for fresh lands saw the much closer Kansas-Nebraska Territory as ripe for development. At the same time the federal government joined with business leaders to investigate rail routes from the Midwest to the Pacific Ocean. A line across the Kansas-Nebraska Territory was logical and strongly advocated by such midwestern senators as Stephen A. Douglas of Illinois. Under Douglas's leadership, the Senate in 1854 looked to Kansas-Nebraska as the next western territory to be settled and organized.

Stephen Douglas was a new breed of senator, different from the older statesmen like Calhoun and Webster. In addition to his political ambitions (he wanted to be president), Douglas had financial ambitions. He hoped to be one of the developers of the first transcontinental railroad. He saw opportunity for himself along the advancing frontier. The quick organization of Kansas and Nebraska, he believed, would aid the nation's progress by providing a route for the transcontinental railroad.

As would be the case time and again with western territory, the prospect of fortunes to be made—this time in transportation and agriculture—caused people to fight and argue bitterly over virgin territory before one farm had been sold or one track had been laid.

Technically, the Kansas-Nebraska area fell within the boundaries of the Louisiana Purchase. By the terms of the Compromise of 1820, any territory within the Louisiana Purchase was to be divided slave and free according to its position south or north of the latitude 36° 30'. It would seem that the issue of slavery in the Kansas-Nebraska Territory would have been easily settled. All of the territory lay above the compromise line, and so, according to the agreement set forth in 1820, it should have been closed to slavery.

If the compromise line were followed, Douglas and others feared that southern senators would delay the organization of the territory indefinitely. In order for the railroads to be built and farms to be settled, the territory needed to be organized by Congress. Douglas, eager to get the matter settled, proposed a bill that he hoped would win support from both Northerners and Southerners. He suggested that the area be organized into two separate territories, Kansas and Nebraska, and that the issue of slavery be settled by the citizens of the territory at a later date. Douglas's bill passed.

As a consequence of Douglas's bill, Kansas and Nebraska, but especially Kansas, earned a bloody chapter in the history of western violence. "Bleeding Kansas" captured headlines as agitators for and against slavery raced into the area. Most famous of these Kansas pioneers was undoubtedly the abolitionist John Brown, who touched off a wave of violence when he and his sons murdered several Kansas settlers with reputations as southern sympathizers. This "Pottawatomie Massacre" led to more civil violence in Kansas, with the result that over two hundred lives were lost. Gunfights and violence seemed to follow the advancing frontier, but this time the objects of the violence were not outlaws or Indians but fellow settlers who disagreed over which parts of eastern civilization should be established in the West.

The majority of the settlers in Kansas had little to do with the conflict. Outside agitators like Brown were more likely to cause the fighting. Very few people migrated to the territory from either the plantation South or abolitionist New England. The census of 1860 showed exactly two slaves living in Kansas, and yet northern members of the Free Soil Party, a party committed to preventing the spread of slavery, argued that Kansas was fast becoming an extension of the "slavocracy." The vast majority of settlers migrated laterally to Kansas from Ohio and Missouri. Nevertheless, to the rest of the nation, it seemed as though the violent West was again leading the country in the direction of civil war.

*A Westerner Leads
the Nation through War*
The burden of leading the nation through the Civil War fell upon Abraham Lincoln, a man who was firmly a part of the western tradition. Abraham Lincoln had been

Abraham Lincoln met Stephen Douglas in a famous debate that established Lincoln as Illinois's leading politician. The signs in the crowd show his appeal to western interests.

born only twenty years after the ratification of the Constitution. He was born in Kentucky when that area had barely achieved statehood. His father was a typical pioneer farmer who moved his family first to Indiana and then to Illinois, always seeking new land, greater success, and a better future for his children. Most American school children can describe Abe Lincoln. In doing so they are very likely to use adjectives typical of descriptions of pioneers: lanky, strong, courageous, honest, and hardworking. Lincoln knew how to spin a yarn, fell a tree, and plow a field, traditional frontier accomplishments.

Like other people born along the advancing frontier, Abraham Lincoln believed in progress. He was typical of westerners, not only by virtue of his physique and his talents, but also by virtue of his values. He believed in success as defined by American capitalism; in fact he was a successful corporate lawyer in Illinois. Like Stephen Douglas, his leading political opponent, he supported the expansion of railroads and believed in government land grants to facilitate this growth.

Lincoln, along with his wife Mary Todd Lincoln, worried about giving his sons the polish and education that eastern boys would have received. In short, he wanted the West to catch up with the East culturally as quickly as possible. Although he allowed his campaign managers to use his log-cabin childhood as a political gimmick, he had no desire to remain in a log cabin once he could afford to live in a grander style. Like most of the westward pioneers, he saw primitive living conditions as an unfortunate, albeit unavoidable, step in the development of new lands. He did not see life in an isolated cabin as a desirable final goal for himself or for any other progressive nineteenth-century American.

When Lincoln was elected to the presidency in 1860, the country was poised on the edge of war. The Whig and Democratic parties, the two leading political factions, had been fragmented by sectional arguments among their northern and southern supporters. Lincoln won the election on the Republican ticket. He did not win a majority of the popular vote, but the split in the electoral college among the many candidates enabled him to capture the office.

Lincoln, like most Republicans, opposed the extension of slavery into the western territories. By 1860 this position was anathema to the South. With the news of Lincoln's election, South Carolina, Calhoun's native state, withdrew from the Union. South Carolina was followed eventually by ten other states. From 1861 until his assassination in 1865, Abraham Lincoln presided over a divided nation. It was his task to prosecute a war that killed nearly as many Americans as all previous American wars combined. Through it all Lincoln had one goal—to reunite the United States.

It is not surprising that the preservation of the Union became Lincoln's guiding principle. He was a child of Manifest Destiny who firmly believed that a Divine Being had ordained that the American flag should fly over the entire continent. The sectional tensions that helped to create the Civil War can be seen as serious growing pains in the final incorporation of the western lands into the nation. In the end, the frontier tradition mandated the outcome of the Civil War—a nation united from Atlantic to Pacific.

5 | The Dark Side of Westward Expansion: Prejudice and Oppression

When the Civil War ended in 1865, the nation was united from coast to coast. Nevertheless, there were many areas that remained unsettled and that still bore the title "frontier." In fact, because of Hollywood's focus on the frontier of the late nineteenth century—the frontier of the cowboy and Indian, the "good guys" and the "bad guys"—the characteristics of the frontier between 1870 and 1900 often overshadow those of earlier frontiers. And, although settlers along the new line of settlement shared many of the positive traits of their forebears, they also shared negative ones as well. Both sets of characteristics would become part of the frontier legacy to America. The settlers continued to be strong, adventuresome, optimistic, and hardworking. They were also greedy, racist, opportunistic, and prejudiced.

Oppression and Native Americans before the Civil War
In the years before the Civil War people had tried to justify slavery with economic arguments. In the land of economic opportunity, too many forms of prejudice were justified in the name of progress. Perhaps the most heinous of these in the western territories was the oppression of Indians. Certainly the image of American settlers battling Indians along the frontier is one that has remained in our national memory. Too often, however, the Indians are portrayed as savage warriors, shedding white blood simply for the thrill of the hunt. In reality the Indians were often sick, starving, and desperate, forced to uproot their families and violate the laws of their culture, all in the name of progress.

From the time the settlers along the Atlantic Coast first began to move inland, the "Indian problem" was listed near the top of frontier concerns. Stated quite simply, the Indian problem was one of land ownership. Indians controlled land that the white settlers wanted. Most Indians did not own land in the British or European sense, but they hunted across specific tribal lands, and they did not want to see trees felled and lands fenced in to create farms. Furthermore, their economic philosophy was at odds with capitalism.

The Indians grew little more than they could use; they traded with each other for necessities they could not produce themselves. The Indians were not motivated by profit. They did not look at the forests and dream of lumber to build great clipper ships. They did not view a waterfall and dream of the factories it could fuel. When they trapped beaver it was to clothe themselves and their families, not to make a fortune in London hat shops. As Tecumseh, the great Shawnee leader, explained in a speech protesting an illegal sale of Indian lands, "until lately . . . this continent all belonged to red men . . . once a happy race, since made miserable by the white people, who are never contented, but always encroaching."

The two ways of life were bound to clash; inevitably, the Indians would lose. They were outnumbered and their weaponry could not resist gunpowder and shotgun shells. Most Americans believed that it was right that the Indians should lose. The early settlers were not only capitalists, but Protestant Christians. They believed that God would support them against the heathen—that is, nonbelieving—"savages." Of course, there were good settlers, motivated to help the Indians share in the Protestant, capitalistic American way of life. Marcus and Narcissa Whitman were examples of this type of missionary settlers. But there were few, if any, early Americans who believed that the Indians should be left alone on their homelands, living their old ways of life.

Frontier battles with Indians were romantic, gory affairs. In the wake of such battles, whether Harrison's fights in Indiana or Jackson's defeat of the Creeks in the Southwest, the American soldiers gained heroic reputations, the Indians were routed, starving and decimated, and settlers flocked into the area to build farms and towns. Between the War of 1812 and the decade of the 1840s, this pattern was repeated again and again. From the 1920s on, at the conclusion of each battle, whole tribes were moved farther west by government order and settled on new, often inferior, lands set aside for that purpose. These reservations, as they came to be called, were strictly controlled by federal agencies. When trouble arose, the army was sent in to quell the disturbance.

In the 1830s a "permanent" line of Indian frontier was drawn west of the Mississippi River in present-day Oklahoma, Kansas, and Nebraska, and the vast majority of Indians living east of that line, whether peaceful or hostile, were forced to move west. In 1840, 100,000 of the 350,000 Indians living west of the line had been born in the East. They had moved there under the terms of such treaties as John Quincy Adams's deal with the Creeks of West Georgia and Andrew Jackson's negotiation with the Cherokee. Adams, in his haste to add Florida to the United States in 1819, had shown little regard for the Indians in that territory.

A decade later the Cherokees won a case against Georgia's encroachment on their territory. In spite of the Supreme Court's ruling, Andrew Jackson, as president, refused to enforce the judicial decision and supported the removal of the well-established Cherokee from their homeland. In fact, in the vast Old Southwest, once populated by the "Five Civilized Tribes," only the Seminoles remained by the end of the 1830s. The Creeks, Cherokees, Choctaws, and Chickasaws had all been relocated on a reservation north of Texas. The Seminoles lived in the Everglades, a region believed to be uninhabitable by white people. By 1842 many Seminoles had joined the other Civilized Tribes in the western Indian Territory.

This displacement of the Indians had been at one and the same time systematic and unplanned. It was systematic in that it was repeated each time white settlement pushed up against an Indian tribe. As Frederic L. Paxson notes in his *History of the American Frontier,* "The history of the United States showed that no white community lived contentedly with an Indian community in its vicinity." The movement of the Indian tribes was unplanned in that the government had no long-range policy in mind. The pattern was to subdue and remove the Indians east of the Mississippi whenever they seemed to be in the way of progress. What to do with them after the land ran out or when white settlement crossed the Mississippi were questions that had not been addressed in the early 1830s.

Many American statesmen had a hand in solving the Indian question. In 1825 Secretary of War John C. Calhoun had recommended to Congress and to President Monroe that the Indians should all be removed to a "tract of country west of the State of Missouri and the Territory of Arkansas." This should be done, he believed, with the "strongest and most solemn assurance that the country given them should be theirs, as a permanent home for themselves and their posterity."

In order for this policy to work, the Indians had to agree to trade their eastern lands for new ones in the West. Once again greed and corruption played unhappy roles in the treaty negotiations and land transfers. Many of the tribes in the East, particularly the Five Civilized Tribes of the Southeast, had adapted to a peaceful, agricultural way of life. They did not want to relinquish the fertile soil of Georgia for the barren lands of Oklahoma. Yet they had no choice. Through swindles and force, they were coerced into relinquishing their land and making the harsh trek west.

The path west taken by these Indians in the 1830s has been called the "Trail of Tears." Older historians, such as Paxson, have taken the stance that the Indians' opposition to the move caused their discomfort and anguish. They argue that the Indians stubbornly resisted progress and so doomed themselves to their fate. A Baptist minister who watched a part of the march had a different view of things. He wrote, "The Cherokees are nearly all prisoners. They have been dragged from their homes . . . multitudes were allowed no time to take anything with them except the clothes they had on. . . . a painful sight." Other sympathetic modern writers, such as Samuel Eliot Morison, have argued that "the process was carried out with unnecessary hardship to the victims." At the time, very few American politicians spoke out against moving law-abiding, peaceful people against their will to new homes. Henry Clay, senator from Kentucky, was an exception. In 1835 he addressed the Senate on the subject of Indian removal, claiming that basic principles of human decency and justice were being violated by the government's treatment of the Indians. Not only were the Indian people having their property illegally taken from them, stated Clay, but a ruling of the Supreme Court was being violated by the executive action.

Clay's appeal did nothing to change the mind of such Indian fighters as Andrew Jackson, who had been elected President of the United States in 1828. Jackson was determined to execute the Indian Removal Act of 1830. This law, passed by Congress, provided money that federal Indian agents could use to buy the lands of those Indians still living in the East. The enforced purchase of their lands caused the Indians to look for new homes. Again government agents stepped in, offering to sell the Indians dry, barren land in the Oklahoma Territory, believed to be useless for white settlement.

Jackson went on public record as maintaining that the only alternative to this Indian removal was the extermination of the Indian tribes. He cared little about the methods employed to remove the Indians from the East as long as the goal was met. Throughout the 1830s he ordered U.S. Army troops to herd the Indians west. In his farewell address upon leaving the presidency in 1837, Jackson declared that the eastern tribes had "retarded improvement"—that is, they had stood in the way of western expansion. He said, "The states which had so long been retarded in their improvement by the Indian tribes residing in the midst of them are at length relieved from the evil." In counting the triumphs of his administration, "Old Hickory," the Indian fighter, listed near the top a policy that effectively resulted in the deaths of thousands of Indians. Outweighing the destruction of the tribe people for Jackson and for most of his fellow citizens were the progress west, the in-

Artist Robert Lindneux captured the pathos of the Cherokee removal in 1838 in this painting, "The Trail of Tears."

creasing civilization of the nation, and the growing wealth of its citizens.

Discrimination against Native Americans after the Civil War

After the Civil War, whites continued to settle the conflict between western expansion and the rights of Native Americans by violating the latter. The treaties moving the Indians into the western plains areas had provided that these new lands would remain in Indian possession for "as long as the grass grows and the rivers run." With the end of the Civil War, however, came a new rush to populate western plains areas that had previously been believed to be unsuitable for white habitation. Once again, treaties were broken, war broke out, and, in the end, the Indians were forced to move to new, inferior lands against their will.

The first hints that the Indians might have to give up their "permanent" tribal lands had actually predated the Civil War. Plans for a transcontinental railroad raised the issue of Indian hunting grounds on the Great Plains. With the introduction of the steam locomotive in the 1840s, the federal government wanted to grant land to private railroad companies in order to speed up the process of linking the East and West by rail. The land they contemplated using for this purpose was held by Indian tribes. As early as 1851 tribal chiefs were called together by the federal government to a meeting. They were told that they would have to limit their hunting expeditions to distinct areas agreed upon with government officials. In this way the hunting parties could be controlled, and armed Indian parties would be less threatening to the railroad builders.

The Civil War stopped the railroad temporarily and focused the nation's attention on the battlefields of the

East. Well before the final gunshot, however, it was clear that the North would win and that the aftermath of the war would bring a resumption of railroad construction. To this end Congress agreed that the Union Pacific would build the first transcontinental line west from Omaha, Nebraska. This line would join one constructed by the Central Pacific running east from California. Of course, this line ran through land belonging to western Indian tribes. In violating Indian treaty agreements, the building of the transcontinental railroad, so highly desired by western pioneers, set off two decades of Indian warfare in which many pioneers and even more Indians lost their lives. In the end the federal armies triumphed over the Native Americans; between 1867 and 1890 100,000 Indians were forced onto reservations. In the course of being pushed onto the reservations, thousands of Indians died of disease, starvation, and gunshot. For example, there were approximately 200,000 Indians living in California the year before the gold rush; by 1900 only 15,000 Indians remained in that state.

The two decades after the Civil War saw the Indian and cowboy conflicts that have lingered in American memory because of movies and novels. This was the era of the Apache, Sioux, and Nez Percé warriors, of Geronimo, Chief Joseph, and Sitting Bull. This was the time of Custer's Last Stand at the Little Bighorn and the Battle of Wounded Knee. Yet colorful and exciting as the images conjured up by these names, the reality was quite different. The late nineteenth century saw not only the closing of the American continental frontier, but also the last chapter in the history of the American Indians as a free, nomadic, hunting people. The victory of the federal government over the Indians in the Sioux Wars of 1890 marked the end. At Wounded

Knee, South Dakota, 200 defenseless men, women, and children of the Sioux nation were killed by federal gunfire. The days of the Indian fighters had come to an end.

Hereafter, Indian battles with the United States would be fought in courts, not on the plains. For a century and more Indians attempted in court to prove that their lands had been wrongfully taken from them. From 1890 on, Indians lost population, and tribal customs were visible only on ceremonial occasions, not as a way of life.

For the Plains Indians the final closing of their frontier arrived three years before the official closing of the frontier as Turner noted it. The Dawes Act of 1887 established the principle that the most desirable living condition for all Indians was on individually owned pieces of land within the reservation, rather than by communal tribal ownership of the reservation land as a whole. For the two decades preceding the passage of this law, Indians had been consolidated into smaller and smaller reservations. Because of their alleged sympathy to the Confederacy during the war, the Five Civilized Tribes that had lived on the Oklahoma reservation since their forced march west in the 1830s had lost their rights to much of their land. The federal government declared that the conduct of these tribes during the war meant that the federal government no longer had to honor its treaty obligations. Sweeping generalizations about Indian conduct during the Civil War did not distinguish between the slave-owning Choctaw and Chickasaw and the Cherokee, many of whom had raised troops to fight on the Union side.

The Dawes Act continued to demonstrate white insensitivity toward individual Indian tribes and their needs. By this act the President of the United States had the right to determine when Indian tribes were civilized enough to become farmers. When that determination was made, land from the tribe's reservation holdings was given to each head of a family. These individuals were to hold the land for twenty-five years to prove that they could manage farms as well as the white man could. After twenty-five years, the farm could pass to the Indian free and clear. Meanwhile, by accepting the land, the head of the family was granted American citizenship.

The Dawes Act attempted to give to western Indians what western white pioneers wanted—land of one's own to farm. What the Dawes Act failed to consider was the Indians' lack of experience with, and lack of interest in, private land ownership. The way of the white farmer was not the way of the American Indian. In fact, the differences between these two ways of life had been at the root of the clash between westward moving farmers and Native Americans since the early colonists began cutting down the forests. Unused to land ownership, the Indians lost much of the land awarded to them under the Dawes Act when individual Indian farmers defaulted on mortgages and their lands reverted to banks and government agencies. In 1887 tribal lands equalled 137 million acres; by 1930 only 50 million acres remained in Indian hands. Some historians have argued that greedy Westerners foresaw this loss of Indian lands as a reason for supporting the Dawes Act. It is far more likely that backers of the Dawes Act acted in good faith, but with no understanding of the Indian culture. The nation was committed to one vision of its destiny. That destiny was believed to be agricultural, industrial, and cultural progress, all defined in terms of nineteenth-century capitalism. There was no place for the communal life of the Indian in such a future.

Immigrants Along the Advancing Frontier
The Indians were not the only group to suffer harsh prejudice in the course of the nation's westward expansion. Immigrants, too, faced discrimination. The nineteenth century saw the influx of thousands of immigrants into the United States each year. Although most of these people landed first in cities, and were often trapped there forever by poverty, some managed to make their way west. In the century between 1820 and 1920, nearly thirty-five million immigrants entered the United States. In the first half of this period, most immigrants came from England, Scotland, Germany, and northern Ireland. In the second half, the immigrant groups displayed a far greater diversity of national origin, religion, and race. Among these later groups, the Scandinavians, the Germans, and the Chinese were most often found in frontier areas.

Regardless of their birthplace, most immigrants had come from an agricultural background in the Old World. Their dreams for their new lives in America were tightly linked to their belief that America was a nation with enough land for all newcomers. Once the immigrants arrived here, their dreams joined those of the flood of Americans moving west.

No other nation in the world welcomed immigrants as warmly as the United States. However, in spite of the national policy of welcome, individuals frequently met with prejudice. There were also places, of course, where immigrants found tolerance and neighborliness. On the frontier, where white neighbors might be scattered miles apart, any companionship was welcomed. In even the most primitive frontier communities, immigrants tended to join together.

Often newcomers migrated to a specific area because relatives or neighbors from the Old Country were already there. As Kenneth Libo and Irving Howe have commented in their study of Jewish pioneers *(We Lived There, Too)*, "As long as there were enough Yiddish-speaking Jews in an American . . . town to form a neighborhood of their own, it was possible to recreate the look and feel of an East European *shtetl* [Jewish village] wherein the values of *Yiddishkeit* [Jewish way of life], far from being abandoned or forgotten, provided direction and meaning to the lives of young and old alike."

In spite of the prejudice against them, European Jews were among the most successful of the western pioneers. Few people could hope to match the success of the immigrant Levi Strauss, who arrived in the United States in 1846, migrated to California during the gold rush years, and by 1880 had sold over 100,000 blue canvas and copper-studded "Levi" overalls and jackets. Similar success stories were those of Meyer Guggenheim of Pueblo, Colorado, whose merchant fortune would one day fund the Guggenheim fellowships, and Mike Goldwater of Phoenix, Arizona, whose grandson, Barry, would run for president, backed by profits from the prosperous family dry goods business established by his grandfather. These individual examples of success, however, need to be balanced against the general feeling of intolerance that most European Jews experienced in western communities. For example, the all-American folk humorist, Mark Twain, in his reminiscences of his boyhood in Hannibal, Missouri, makes matter-of-fact anti-Semitic remarks typical of his time.

The Chinese, like the Indians and Jews, met a very hostile reception in western communities. Thousands of Chinese migrated to California at the time of the gold rush. Not only were their skin color, language and customs different from those of American prospectors, the Chinese did not intend to settle in California. Most were single young men who planned to return to China once they had made their fortunes.

Prejudice against immigrant groups undermines Turner's belief that the frontier produced a purer democracy than had been possible in England or in early cities along the East Coast. In fact, in reproducing eastern society as quickly as possible, the frontier people often reproduced the flaws of the East as well as eastern virtues. Turner and his adherents viewed the frontier as a place where Europeans became Americans through their contact with a harsh environment. True as this may be, it is also true that the Anglo- and German-American pioneers decided which of the foreign born could become American. Job discrimination, unequal pay scales for groups such as the Chinese, housing discrimination and education geared to the English-speaking created a society in which the older, well-established groups maintained control of politics and the economy.

Scandinavians in the Midwest, Irish along the railroad route, Chinese in California, and Mexicans throughout the Southwest faced discrimination and intolerance. In addition to battling frontier conditions, these people had to fight hostile prejudice that was unneighborly at best and life threatening at its worst. The forms of this prejudice ranged from schoolboys' taunts at Chinese "pigtails" to bankers' refusals to extend credit to Norwegians unable to speak English. However, in states like Wisconsin where the numbers of new immigrants—in this case, Scandinavians—soon outnumbered the other settlers, acceptance came much more rapidly.

The Mormons—
Another Form of Prejudice
No account of westward expansion and prejudice is complete without mentioning the Mormons. On the one hand, this small, but hardy, religious group was the victim of prejudice time and time again. On the other hand, their success story is the quintessential success story of a minority group in America and of the conquering of nature by determined pioneers.

In 1830 the Mormon Church was founded by Joseph Smith; by 1865 one thousand miles of irrigation, laid by Mormons, had transformed the desert around the Great Salt Lake into productive farm country, and by 1896 Utah was a state. The story of the settlement of Utah is inextricably bound up with the story of Smith and his religion.

Joseph Smith was living in the small western New York town of Palmyra when he allegedly discovered a set of gold plates upon which were heiroglyphic writings which he translated into the *Book of Mormon,* a volume that became the cornerstone of history for God's "chosen people." According to Smith's translation of these plates, God sent a tribe of the Israelites to North America. The survivors of this tribe settled near Palmyra about A.D. 450 and buried the teachings of their leader, Mormon, on a hill where they awaited discovery by Joseph Smith, a disciple chosen by God.

This history of the Mormons met with widespread derision, but a few people became fervent believers. In 1830 the Church of Jesus Christ of the Latter Day Saints was organized on Morman principles with Smith as its spiritual leader. In addition to the *Book of Mormon,* Smith also wrote the *Doctrine and Covenants,* the book which laid down rules for daily Mormon living. Many of these rules were communal, including the highly controversial laws regarding community ownership of property. Most nineteenth-century Americans believed in private ownership of property with an almost religious fervor. The Mormons' advocacy of group ownership seemed un-American and even un-Christian. The combination of beliefs and debts that he had incurred and could not pay led Smith to flee to Missouri in 1838.

Smith chose Missouri because a sizable group of his followers had formed in this state. However, Missouri in 1838 was a frontier area beset with local prejudice and narrow-mindedness. During the winter of 1838–39 over fifteen thousand Mormons were driven from Missouri by hostile and self-righteous Missouri citizens who were especially upset that the Mormons allowed Indians to join their church. Frederick Merk has said of the Mormons' harassment: "This was one of the most disgraceful instances of religious intolerance and persecution in American history."

Under Smith's leadership the Mormons fled to Nauvoo, Illinois, where they prospered for a time, and their numbers grew. Then in 1843 Smith received yet another revelation from God, one that enraged the citizens of Illinois. According to Smith, God had approved of polygamy among the Mormons (that is, Mormon men could have several wives). When this news was made public, Smith was killed. A new leader, Brigham Young, arranged for the other Mormons to leave Illinois peacefully, provided they left soon.

As Young looked to the West, he knew that he could not take his followers to California or to Oregon because he would find the same hostility there that he had found in Missouri and Illinois. What the Mormons needed, because of the prejudice they faced, was to find isolation from the other Americans. With this in mind, Young and other Mormon leaders settled upon the land surrounding the Great Salt Lake, a land that had been bypassed because of its aridity as hurriedly as possible by other western travelers.

In the summer of 1847, the first Mormon group reached the Great Salt Lake. Almost immediately they began to lay out the city of the future—Salt Lake City. In doing this they repeated the pattern of all other pioneer groups. They wished to build a future of prosperity and growth. As Alexander B. Adams describes in *The Disputed Lands*, "This was to be no ramshackle frontier settlement, but a well laid-out, dignified city." The communal laws of Mormonism worked to their advantage. Together they irrigated the land by diverting streams from the nearby Wasatch Range, together they fought the plagues of locusts threatening their crops, and together they built their city and its great temple. With the rush of forty-niners to the gold fields of California came a new source of wealth for the Mormons: they became suppliers for adventurers and prospectors making the trek west.

Most of these westward travelers did not stop long in Utah, but continued west. Because of prejudice, the Mormons had drawn apart from the frontier mainstream. By the strength of their numbers, they were able to continue their way of life, prosper, and remain separate. When the Utah Territory was organized in 1850, its first governor was Brigham Young. Not until Utah's application for statehood in the 1890s would the Mormon way of life come under major scrutiny. By then

GOOD NEWS
FOR
MINERS.

NEW GOODS,
PROVISIONS, TOOLS,
CLOTHING, &c. &c.

GREAT BARGAINS!
JUST RECEIVED BY THE SUBSCRIBERS, AT THE LARGE TENT ON THE HILL,

A superior Lot of New, Valuable and most DESIRABLE GOODS for Miners and for residents also. Among them are the following:

STAPLE PROVISIONS AND STORES.

Pork, Flour, Bread, Beef, Hams, Mackerel, Sugar, Molasses, Coffee, Teas, Butter & Cheese, Pickles, Beans, Peas, Rice, Chocolate, Spices, Salt, Soap, Vinegar, &c.

EXTRA PROVISIONS AND STORES.

Every variety of Preserved Meats and Vegetables and Fruits, [more than eighty different kinds.] Tongues and Sounds; Smoked Halibut; Dry Cod Fish; Eggs fresh and fine; Figs, Raisins, Almonds and Nuts; China Preserves; China Bread and Cakes; Butter Crackers, Boston Crackers, and many other very desirable and choice bits.

DESIRABLE GOODS FOR COMFORT. AND HEALTH.

Patent Cot Bedsteads, Mattresses and Pillows, Blankets and Comforters. Also, in Clothing—Overcoats, Jackets, Miner's heavy Velvet Coats and Pantaloons, Woolen Pants, Guernsey Frocks, Flannel Shirts and Drawers, Stockings and Socks, Boots, Shoes; Rubber Waders, Coats, Blankets, &c.

MINING TOOLS, &c.; BUILDING MATERIALS, &c.

Cradles, Shovels, Spades, Hoes, Picks, Axes, Hatchets, Hammers; every variety of Workman's Tools, Nails, Screws, Brads, &c.

SUPERIOR GOLD SCALES.   MEDICINE CHESTS, &c.

Superior Medicine Chests, well assorted, together with the principal Important Medicines for Dysentery, Fever and Fever and Ague, Scurvy, &c.

N.B.—Important Express Arrangement for Miners.

The Subscribers will run an EXPRESS to and from every Steamer, carrying and returning Letters for the Post Office and Expresses to the States. Also, conveying "GOLD DUST" or Parcels, to and from the Mines to the Banking Houses, or the several Expresses for the States, insuring their safety.——The various NEWSPAPERS, from the Eastern, Western and Southern States, will also be found on sale at our stores, together with a large stock of BOOKS and PAMPHLETS constantly on hand.

Excelsior Tent, Mormon Island,
January 1, 1850.   ALTA CALIFORNIA PRESS.   **WARREN & CO.**

A Mormon shopkeeper at the Mormon Island Emporium advertised his miners supplies with this broadside in 1850.

polygamy had been outlawed by federal statute (the Edmunds Act of 1882), and, on paper at least, the church fathers were willing to sacrifice this tenet of their religion to the greater good of Utah's acceptance as a state.

The history of the Mormons contains within it all of the elements of the story of westward expansion. Prejudice is there; in addition to being victims of the most violent discrimination, the Mormons, themselves, were guilty of anti-black teachings. The Mormons taught that blacks were a lesser race and were not entitled to membership in the Mormon church. Material success is there; the Mormons prospered and Utah became the most highly developed agricultural state in the Great Basin. Innovation is there; the Mormons were the first white settlers to irrigate the desert extensively and successfully. The Mormons were strong, hardworking, and visionary. They looked at a desert and saw a city. They were American pioneers.

Prejudice and discrimination are as much a part of the history of westward expansion as they are of the history of the South or the history of northeastern ghettos. That frontier democracy was tinged with racial and ethnic prejudice does not erase the fact that democracy for the majority did exist on the edge of civilization. That some pioneers were held back from success because of religion, color, and place of origin does not alter the success of thousands of others. But in studying the westward expansion of the United States, as in studying any other phase of the nation's history, it is important to include the darker side of people's motives and actions. For, in learning about the hostility and prejudice faced by some pioneers comes a greater respect for those who forged democracy again and again as they moved the country westward.

6

Cowboys and Miners: The Wild, Wild West

The settlers who moved west were mostly farmers searching for new lands on which to establish new and better farms for their families. Their trek began as soon as the villages of Plymouth, Massachusetts, and Jamestown, Virginia, grew too small to provide new acreage. Dominant as these farmers should be in the history of the westward movement, two other groups have far outshadowed them in the nation's memory. In the minds of many Americans the history of the advancing frontier is a story of violence and lawlessness. Since the publication of Owen Wister's *The Virginian* in 1902, the image of the violent Wild West has been an important aspect of the nation's identity. Cowboys and miners dominate these legends. The romance of a West peopled by the very, very good and the very, very bad is a powerful tonic, expecially in an age when heroes and heroines are hard to find and their fame is fleeting.

Gold and Silver on the Frontier
In the summer of 1848, while building a mill for his employer John Sutter, a man named James Marshall discovered gold in the riverbed where he was working. Although the news of this discovery traveled very slowly at first, by the end of 1848 eighty thousand people had flooded California looking for gold, and by 1849 a true "gold rush" had begun. Fifty thousand people moved west along the California trail in that one year alone. In 1849 gold sold for nearly twenty dollars an ounce; ten million ounces were mined from the California gold

fields that year. By 1852 there were one hundred thousand prospectors mining in California.

What began with gold in California would be continued with the discovery of other precious metals in other western states. In 1859 silver was discovered in the hills of Nevada at the famous Comstock Lode. The silver discovery brought a new word into the American vernacular—bonanza. A bonanza was any large discovery of very rich ore. More bonanzas would follow with the discovery of copper, silver, and lead in Colorado in the 1870s, the discovery of copper in the Anaconda area near Butte, Montana, in the 1880s, and, in the last major mining discovery in the forty-eight contiguous states, the discovery of gold near Cripple Creek, Colorado.

All of these discoveries brought instant fame to towns that passed into American legend and song. Cripple Creek, Deadwood, Tombstone, Virginia City, and Alder Gulch were all born on the mining frontier. This was a frontier that, unlike its predecessors, moved east. After the initial California rush, the miners moved back to Nevada, Idaho, Montana, and Arizona. In 1850 the influx of miners was responsible for California's quick readiness for statehood. Miners contributed similarly to Idaho's territorial status in 1863 and Nevada's statehood in 1864. And, with the surge of population from mining in that area in the 1870s, Colorado became the centennial state in 1876.

As the historian Harvey Carter has pointed out, the mining frontier was urban in character right from the beginning, as prospectors and their money gave rise to boomtowns. "Forty-niners," miners who headed west at the time of the California gold rush, tended to be young men between the ages of twenty and thirty, and other mining populations probably fit this profile as well.

A wagon train circles on the main street of Denver, Colorado, in 1868.

They were full of energy, physical strength, exuberance, and confidence. Overnight they built towns that matched their character. As Ray A. Billington has written, "Wherever [they] went, they left behind a residue of camps that served as magnets for capital; this in turn attracted workers, farmers to feed those workers, merchants to supply the farmers, and the dozens of others needed to plant the seeds of civilization." Echoes Marvin Louis in his *Mining Frontier*, "The mining frontier brought in its wake sporadic outbursts of prosperity, progress and disorder . . . [and] a cultural diversity."

The miners transformed the older towns of the West at the same time that their numbers gave rise to new ones. San Francisco boomed. Joseph Revere observed of that city in 1849, "The little idle place that I had left . . . was now, by the potent power of gold, metamorphized into a canvas city of several thousand people." Billington describes the silver capital of Virginia City, Nevada, in 1863 in these words: "[It] was a booming metropolis of 15,000 souls with an opera house, three theatres, restaurants that rivalled those of San Francisco, and ornate saloons where bearded miners could quaff champagne rather than the 'tarantula juice' and 'Tangle Leg Whiskey' in which they had drowned their troubles only a few years before."

The mining frontier revolutionized communication with and transportation to the West. The image of the miner as a mule-loving, tobacco-spitting illiterate is a false one, if the proliferation of newspapers in mining areas is any measure of literacy. By 1856, for example, there were eighty-nine newspapers published in California alone. In 1849 there had been one. The miners, like so many other western pioneers, had a strong desire to stay in touch with the East. In their case the need was even greater than it was for western farmers.

Miners depended on news of gold and silver prices on eastern and European markets. In addition, they frequently needed the backing of the eastern financial community.

Initially, prospectors were able to mine their gold by the placer or panning method. They would scoop up a panful of dirt and run it through a sieve. If chunks of gold were present, they would remain when the water and silt had washed out. When this happened, the miner was said to have "hit paydirt." Once the surface deposits were depleted, however, miners needed financial support to buy the equipment needed to continue their mining.

For a miner to be successful, he needed to go more deeply into the veins of the mineral deposits than placer mining would allow. Hydraulic mining and shaft mining required large outlays of capital. The money for such ventures lay with bankers back East, and the miners had to be able to communicate with these men. Successful mining was an expensive undertaking. Of all the people who headed west to find fortunes, very few struck it rich in the mines. Many fortunes were made, however, as failed prospectors turned to supplying their more fortunate friends with equipment, food, and drink.

Mining and Transportation
The mining frontier stimulated a revolution in western transportation. The earliest pioneers had followed buffalo trails to cross the mountains. Succeeding pioneers had beaten down these paths so that wagon trains could use them, but the trip was still exceedingly slow. Mail sent by wagon train took several months to reach the West Coast. In 1857 Congress authorized the postmaster general to spend $600,000 annually to contract with

Digging for gold in California

a company for semiweekly mail delivery that would take no longer than twenty-five days to reach San Francisco from Tipton, Missouri, at that time the western terminus of the railroad. Competing firms vied for the contract. Butterfield Overland Mail firm and Pike's Peak Express Company (founder of the Pony Express system) were early competitors. By 1866 Wells Fargo had driven all the other companies out of business.

Although the Pony Express was dramatic and romantic, Wells Fargo quickly replaced these lone riders with stagecoach runs. Pony Express riders had carried the mail nearly two thousand miles, traveling on the average six and a half miles per hour. The Concord coaches favored by Wells Fargo were somewhat slower, but in addition to the mail they carried passengers. The leather thoroughbraces under the coach were designed to allow the coach to sway rather than bounce, but the trip was still arduous and uncomfortable. Alexander Adams quotes a passenger disembarking from a stagecoach in 1859 as saying, "I know what hell is like. I've had twenty four days of it."

Like the Pony Express, the overland stage journey was short lived. The railroad was coming. The Central Pacific and the Union Pacific joined the country's rail lines together at Promontory, Utah, in 1869. Within twenty years, five more railroads would crisscross the country: the Southern Pacific, the Santa Fe, the Oregon Short Line, the Northern Pacific, and the Great Northern. The development of the mining frontier, with its promise of great wealth for the country, had encouraged Congress to support rapid construction of these railroads.

Over 75 percent of the land authorized for sale by the Homestead Act of 1862 ended up as railroad land grants. Instead of providing land for individual farmers as the law had originally intended, Congress voted again and again to grant large parcels of the available land to railroad companies. By giving the land for railroad construction to the rail companies, Congress sped up the process of building the rail lines. At the same time the grants enabled the railroad companies to make exorbitant profits and to take advantage of the farm settlers living alongside the railroad routes. Since the companies did not have to buy the land, one of the greatest costs in building a new railroad was avoided. Rather than pass these savings on to the farmers along their routes, the railroads used their land as a way of making even more money. They sold or rented parcels on either side of the tracks to citizens at a much higher rate than the federal government would have charged under the terms of the Homestead Act. The gold rush had touched off a fever that spread to other parts of the nation's economy. Whether in gold, silver, or railroads, the post–Civil War era was a time for "get-rich-quick" schemes.

Violence on the Mining Frontier
The mining frontier was certainly a part of the "Gilded Age" of American capitalism. The decades of the 1870s and 1880s earned this term because of the fortunes that seemed to be made overnight. Along the frontier, quick fortunes were also associated with violence and greed. Were the miners themselves, or the towns they constructed, any more lawless or violent than any other sectors of the frontier? They certainly seemed so, and their legends have reinforced this image. Claim-jumping, shoot-outs, feuds, high-stake poker games, and swinging saloon doors are all an indelible part of Hollywood's portrait of the mining frontier.

The reality, however, may have been somewhat

different. The mining towns grew so quickly that, in Harvey Carter's words, "[they] crudely reproduced the vices less overt in more slowly growing cities." For example, there was much violence against labor unions in all parts of America before 1900, but in the silver and copper mining areas this violence was most prevalent. Discrimination against the foreign-born existed in all eastern cities in the 1870s and 1880s, but in mining towns, hostility toward Chinese and Indians seemed particularly violent and ugly.

On the plus side, a number of states along the mining frontier first offered political equality to women. In an odd way, the violence associated with mining life led to the movement for votes for women in both Wyoming and Colorado. As Esther Morris, a leading Wyoming suffragist, saw it, women's votes would be a civilizing influence in a state badly in need of law and order. For whatever reasons, when the men of Wyoming appealed to Congress for statehood, they asserted, "We may stay out of the Union for one hundred years, but we will come in with our women." By 1893 women could vote in Colorado, and Idaho enfranchised women in 1896. What Julie Roy Jeffrey in *Frontier Women* calls the "pioneer determination to turn wilderness into civilization" led not only to votes for women, but in Wyoming at least, to a married woman's property law (enabling women to keep their property in their own names even after marriage) and a bill for equal pay for women teachers. Contact with the frontier and its harshness had indeed led to a widening of democracy.

The Cowboy's Frontier
Boomtowns, quick fortunes, colorful characters, and dramatic violence were all part of the mining frontier

to a certain extent in reality and to a large extent in legend. Only one other group in the westward movement surpasses the prospector in American folklore. To many Americans and perhaps to even more foreigners, the cowboy and his frontier, the range, are synonymous with the United States itself.

Again, reality differs somewhat from the legend. Far from dominating the country's westward expansion, the cowboy in his true form existed for only thirty years, from the 1860s to the 1890s. During those three decades the cattle drive was born and died, and true cowboys came into the West and passed from it.

In the early 1860s a few enterprising Westerners noted the presence in Texas of approximately five million wild cattle—the famous Texas longhorns. These beeves sold for three to five dollars a head in the Southwest. Back East they were worth ten times that much. The problem was to find a way to get these cattle from Texas to the cities of the Northeast. The solution was found after the Civil War.

In March, 1866, the first herds began the trek north to market along the Chisholm Trail. These cattle were driven by cowboys, riders who were hired to herd the beasts, called mavericks because they were unbranded, from Texas to the railroad terminus in Abilene, Kansas. Here the cattle would be fattened and sold to dealers for the trip by rail to eastern markets. It was also here at Abilene that the cowboys received their pay—and often spent it in a few days of fun and frolic—before heading, usually penniless, back to the Texas ranches from which the whole process would begin the next spring. Between 1868 and 1871 over one and a half million cattle passed through Abilene.

Abilene was the first and one of the most famous of the cow towns. Like the legendary mining camps,

*A herd of Texas longhorns is driven
to market in Dodge City, Kansas.*

cow towns like Abilene, and later Dodge City, Wichita, and Cheyenne, earned a place in the national mythology. They were crude, raw cities that grew up overnight. Their businesses catered to the cowboy, his paycheck, and his desire for fun and companionship after the loneliness of the trail. Like the mining towns, the cow towns' violence was exaggerated by their newness. In addition to cowboys, most of whom were in town for a very short stay, the cow towns were peopled with bankers and storekeepers, sober citizens who saw the cattle drive as yet another way to make a fortune as the nation moved west.

As profitable as the "Long Drive" seemed, it was not a sound system. The cattle lost too much weight on the trip north, and in traveling from Texas to Kansas, the cowboys had to herd their animals through hostile Indian territory. Furthermore, the annual spring drives meant that too many of the beeves arrived at the market at the same time. This abundant supply depressed cattle prices.

To compensate for those factors, ranchers began driving herds north in order to stock the plains around the railroad centers. In this way ranching spread through Texas, Nebraska, Kansas, and eastern Colorado. Throughout the 1870s and 1880s the ranchers ruled the plains. On occasion they found themselves in conflict with farmers, but in general, ranchers won out during those years. Farmers resented the long drive across their fields and attempted to put up property boundaries, for example barbed wire fences, around their lands. For twenty years, however, the herding business was so good that the wealthy ranchers controlled the western states.

Unusually good weather helped maintain the ranchers' prosperity during the first years of the 1880s.

There was abundant rainfall that kept the grassland plentiful even in areas of serious overgrazing. Disaster struck in 1886 and 1887. A blistering summer scorched the land, and a crippling winter destroyed thousands of the surviving heads of cattle. By 1890 the herds had diminished so severely and the grasslands were so depleted that the years of the open range were over. As William W. Savage, Jr. points out in *Cowboy Hero*, the cowboy lived on in the American mind long after his job had ended. In Savage's words, "He represents rugged individualism . . . unadorned masculinity . . . and ultimate heroism."

The cowboy and the prospector are both important characters in the history of western expansion. They are male heroes with reputations for strength, for courage, and for operating in new territories beyond the reach of conventional law enforcement agencies. It is this last trait that colors the image of their West, and it is this last trait that has recently come under careful scrutiny by historians. As Roger D. McGrath has written in *Gunfighters, Highwaymen and Vigilantes:* "It is popularly assumed that the frontier was full of . . . brave, strong, and reckless men who often resorted to violence—and that these men made the frontier a violent and lawless place."

Certainly this is true in the cowboy legends. Cowboys and prospectors are frequently confused with gunslingers and outlaws. The good guys and the bad guys lived together in the West, runs the common story, and they settled their differences by gunfire. In this mythic West good men were very, very good and bad men were the essence of evil. From the dime novels of the late nineteenth century to John Wayne movies, the images are the same. Women had similar extreme categories—pure or prostitute. Calamity Jane, Wyatt Earp,

The real face of the American cowboy is seen in this photograph from the late 1800s.

Wild Bill Hickok on the side of the law and Belle Starr, Billy the Kid, and the James Brothers on the outlaw side epitomize the types of characters who fought violently on both sides of the law.

But how typical were these people of the frontier dwellers, even in the 1870s, heyday of the cowboy? Recent scholarship indicates that the notorious were exceptions. In a comparison of two Wild West boomtowns—Bodie, Colorado, and Aurora, Nevada—Roger McGrath has found that modern crime problems—theft, burglary, and rape, for example—were virtually nonexistent. By comparing police statistics, he concludes that in the 1870s a person was more likely to be robbed in Boston, Massachusetts, than in Bodie, Colorado. He hypothesizes that the frontier town was full of people with hope for the future and that this optimism served as a deterrent to crime. Accidental gun-related deaths were numerous, but not unexpectedly so in an area heavily populated by young males, all of whom carried firearms and many of whom drank heavily.

The frontier of the miner and the cowboy, then, was a place of adventure and some danger, but not the gratuitous violence that Hollywood and television westerns have led us to believe. It is important for the historians of western expansion to keep the gunslinging part of the frontier story in perspective.

7 Settling the Plains: The Closing of the Continental Frontier

Simultaneous with the development of the mining and ranching frontier, but far more significant for the nation in the long run was the population explosion onto the Great Plains. For years pioneers moving to the West Coast had ignored the possibility of settlement on the Plains. These semiarid, vast fields seemed totally unsuitable for farming, and farmers, after all, made up the bulk of the people moving west.

The land that the California and Oregon pioneers passed up was a huge tract, equal in size to one-fifth the land area of the entire continental United States. In time it would become "the most important single piece of agricultural terrain in the world," as Russell McKee points out in *The Last West*. Until the 1860s, however, this area, known as the Great Plains, was seen as an obstacle, not an opportunity. The trip across the Plains was long, tiring, hot, and filled with danger.

Early Explorers on the Plains
From the days of the Spanish explorers, the Plains had been dismissed as uninhabitable. In the sixteenth century Francisco Vasquez de Coronado explored the panhandle of Texas, traveling through Oklahoma to central Kansas. He called this area *Llano Estacado* or "Staked Plain." Later, French fur traders were the first white people to complete a crossing of the Plains as they searched for new furs. The Comanche and Apache Indians controlled the Plains, and until the 1860s, few white people were allowed in by these natives. The exceptions were the guides and trappers of the first half of the nineteenth century, legendary figures such as

Jim Bridger and Kit Carson. These Plainsmen, in the words of McKee, "could fight, hide behind buffalo grass, walk, endure days of thirst, eat raw meat, drink blood, make such clothing as they needed, wrestle bears, survive snake bites, extract arrows from their bodies." Their lives were romantic and colorful, but hardly an advertisement for farm families to settle on the Plains.

At the conclusion of the Civil War, several factors combined to make the Great Plains the next, and last, desirable continental frontier. First, this was the only large area left. The country was filled in from the Atlantic to the Mississippi and along the West Coast from California to Washington State. Second, the federal army, having subdued the Confederacy, turned to the business of rounding up the Plains Indians onto reservations. Third, the railroad's coming meant that crops grown in the Great Plains states could now get to markets back East. Finally, a host of new inventions allowed farmers to break through the tough grass of the Plains to reach the rich soil underneath.

The Agricultural Revolution and the Great Plains

Between 1870 and 1890 a revolution in agricultural technology took place. Gang plows, disk harrows, grain drills, cord binders, headers, steam threshers—these machines and many more became standard agricultural equipment during the Gilded Age. The new machinery opened up the possibility of productive farm life on the Great Plains.

A farm family that had once been able to cultivate 7 acres of land alone could now manage 135 acres. What no machine could guarantee was adequate rainfall, freedom from blizzards, high winds, and dust storms, escape from plagues of locusts, or relief from loneliness. The pioneers who settled the Plains were an especially courageous group of people. The improvements in technology and transportation might make it seem that their risks were far less than those of their ancestors who first crossed the Appalachians or set out for Oregon Territory. However, the dangers they faced, the challenges they met, and the isolation they endured were intense and unyielding. From their experiences came the most productive agricultural area on earth and earned for the Great Plains the nickname, "Breadbasket for the World."

Even before the Civil War ended, Republican congressmen, anticipating both a victory for the Union and the coming of the railroad, initiated new legislation designed to attract settlers to the Plains. Until this time settlers had continued to be able to purchase 160 acres of government land at the low price of $1.25 per acre. To make government land purchases even more attractive, the federal government passed the Homestead Act in 1862. Under the terms of this act, any head of a household (including immigrants who intended to become citizens) could purchase 160 acres of land for a very small fee (usually around $5.00). The purchaser was required to settle on the land and cultivate it for a minimum of five years. After that, the homestead belonged to the farmer.

There were many farsighted advantages to the Homestead Act. Not least of these was the fact that women as well as men could become homesteaders. This provision spawned two positive results. First, families were able to double their holdings when both the husband and wife filed claims. In an area as dry as the Great Plains, it was often necessary to own a farm larger than 160 acres in order to insure access to sufficient amounts of water. Second, there were many widows and single women who now had the opportunity to farm for themselves, instead of remaining dependent on male relatives. It has been estimated that by 1890 a quarter of a million women were running their own farms and ranches throughout the United States.

In addition to the Homestead Act, Congress also passed the Morrill Land Grant Act in the same year. Under the Morrill Act each state was guaranteed 30,000 acres of federal land per member of Congress to be sold by the state for the purpose of raising money to endow technological and agricultural colleges for that state's citizens. These land-grant colleges, among them Texas A. & M., the University of Nebraska, and the University of Wisconsin, were vital centers in the growth of the Plains states. Not only did they serve as intellectual and cultural centers for their communities, but they also provided inexpensive higher education for farm children. Perhaps most important, through their agricultural stations they furnished information to farmers about crops, climate, and technology that kept American agriculture in the forefront of modern farming.

In spite of the stimulus to settlement created by the federal legislation of the 1860s, it would be a mistake, as Ray Billington has warned, to view the Great Plains as an area of land "free for the asking." The railroads still controlled 180,000 acres of choice land which they sold more often to speculators than to farmers, always for the highest price they could command. And, in addition to the land distributed under the Homestead Act, the federal government continued to sell land at auction and to give out parcels of land as part of the package of Civil War veterans' benefits. In the high-rolling, uncontrolled economy of the Gilded Age, such land sales were always open to speculation, graft, and corruption.

Life on the Great Plains
The farm families who migrated to the Great Plains found an initial problem that had not handicapped earlier pioneers. On the grasslands of the Plains, there was little timber. Without lumber it was difficult to build homes. Demonstrating the innovation that had characterized Westerners on many frontiers, these farmers used what was at hand to construct novel housing. They built their prairie homes from the sod. As one woman, Flora Dutcher, wrote: "My father was one of the early homesteaders in . . . Nebraska. . . . If he looked toward Kansas, what did he see? He saw nothing but sod. If he looked to the north, what did he see? He saw the sod. In all directions what did he see? He saw the sod. Consequently he used the sod to build his home."

Building a sod hut was hard work. Using one of the new steel plows, the farmer cut deeply into the land, digging up thick sod strips. These strips were then laid on top of each other, much the way logs would have been. To keep them together the prairie farmer used a mud paste concocted from water, grass, and dirt. Often the roofs of sod houses bloomed with grass and flowers, but until the railroad could bring better building materials to the Plains these sod huts provided snug protection against blizzards, dust storms and summer heat. For the new settler they were inexpensive. A typical Nebraska sod hut in the late 1880s cost less than fifteen dollars, with most of the money going to tar paper, nails, and lumber for windows and doors.

Two natural problems confronting the pioneer farmers on the Great Plains found solutions that changed the look of the countryside. In the first place, the farmer had to be able to reach water that in many cases lay as far as two hundred feet below the ground's surface.

Windmills had long been used to draw water from the ground; improvements made in the 1870s enabled steel windmills powered by prairie winds to lift water from far below the earth's surface.

Fencing their large pastures posed a second problem for the prairie farmers. Livestock grazed over many acres, but needed to be contained in some way. Joseph Glidden solved this problem with the invention of barbed wire in 1873. By 1880, over eighty million pounds of barbed wire were sold annually in the West. The one drawback of the new wire was the friction it caused throughout the 1880s as farmers fenced in the land over which the cowboys wanted to drive their herds. The end of the Long Drive at the conclusion of the decade put a stop to this hostility for the most part. In the meantime the ranchers turned to such organizations as the extralegal Live-Stock Association to protect their range rights. Occasionally, this protection took the form of gunfire.

By 1890 approximately five million people made their homes on the Great Plains. Wheat had become the area's primary crop. In fewer than thirty years, the time needed to harvest one acre of wheat had dropped from sixty hours to three hours. This great wave of western farmers had succeeded in closing the continental frontier. Between 1867 and the turn of the century, Nebraska, Colorado, North and South Dakota, Montana, Washington, Idaho, Wyoming, and Utah were granted statehood.

The Literature of the Great Plains
For some reason, perhaps because the settlement of the Plains marked the end of the imagined expanse of limitless land, the literature of the last group of pioneers is far less optimistic than that of earlier settlers. Daniel

A family in Custer County, Nebraska, poses in front of their sod house around 1890.

Boone and John Charles Frémont and the cowboy on the Long Drive and the prospector in Cripple Creek had faced life-threatening challenges in their quests to move the boundaries of the nation ever farther westward. However, their accounts of their travels were filled with optimism and hope.

The literature of the Plains, however, is very different. Writers like Willa Cather, Hamlin Garland, and O.E. Rolvaag earned their spots in the galaxy of the nation's great writers by chronicling the depression, loneliness, and hardship of the Plains. Hamlin Garland, who grew up on the Great Plains, wrote of his birthplace in *Main-Traveled Roads:* "Mainly [the road] is long and wearyful, and has a dull little town at one end and a home of toil at the other. Like the main-traveled road of life, it is traversed by many classes of people, but the poor and the weary predominate." For western travelers the road had always been "long and wearyful," but until the settling of the Plains, the end of the road had promised wealth and new opportunity.

"Sooners" Open the Last Territory
By 1889 only the lands of the Oklahoma Territory remained uninhabited by white farmers. The Indian reservations in this area served as a deterrent to white settlement. By executive order in 1885 President Grover Cleveland declared that the Oklahoma District, an area of federal land surrounded by the reservation lands of twenty-two tribes, be opened to settlers in 1889.

The rush of settlers into Oklahoma at noon on April 22, 1889, has been the subject of many novels and movies. Within the first day nearly ten thousand people had established claims. Many, called "Sooners," jumped the gun and entered the territory before the official opening. Their hunger for land highlights the

On April 22, 1889, ten thousand homesteaders rode into Oklahoma to stake their claims to the last open land in the United States.

imminent closing of the frontier. What is frequently omitted from fictitious accounts of the rush into Oklahoma is the continued settlement of this area at the expense of the Indians. Long after April 22, 1889, the federal government continued to sell to white farmers and speculators land that had once belonged to the Indians. Indians were pushed onto smaller and smaller reservation areas. The tide of white farm settlers could not be stopped. In 1907 Oklahoma became the first territory to achieve statehood in the twentieth century.

The Great Plains, then, marked the end of that phase of the nation's westward expansion that had begun in the 1600s. In settling the Plains, the American immigrant farmers demonstrated many of the qualities that had distinguished westward pioneers from the beginning—a sense of adventure, strength, self-reliance, adaptability, innovation, and materialism. At the same time they were sobered by the realization that their frontier was the last. Their exuberance was tinged with a pessimism and a realism that had been missing in their forebears.

8 Beyond the Continental Frontiers

The rush of people into the Oklahoma Territory may have signaled the end of the frontier in the continental United States, but throughout the twentieth century Americans would continue their quests for new frontiers. As late as 1960, the youngest man ever to be elected president, John F. Kennedy, captured the imagination of the country with his slogan, "The New Frontier." It seemed fitting that the young, vital president would associate himself with a young, vital period in American history.

New horizons in medicine, in technology, and in space are frequently referred to as frontiers. For Americans it seems that each new barrier to be hurdled is connected to a past in which seemingly insurmountable barriers were overcome to make the nation. In the second half of the twentieth century two new states entered the Union, Alaska and Hawaii. Neither was directly connected to the landmass comprising the forty-eight states, but both had frontiers that were direct heirs of the tradition of westward expansion.

Hawaii
The settling of Hawaii by white Americans had many of the elements of mainland pioneer settlement stories. There were natives to be Christianized and hardy missionaries eager to do the job. There were fortunes to be made and luxuriant natural resources to be squandered.

Much of Hawaii's early white settlement took place at the same time that pioneers were pushing west on the North American continent. The first group of white settlers, missionaries from New England, arrived in

Hawaii in 1820. The journey had taken five months by sea around Cape Horn. The people who owned and occupied Hawaii were Polynesians, whose culture differed dramatically from that of New England Protestants. The natives wore little clothing, worshipped idols, and were ruled by chiefs who practiced bigamy and incest. Ordinarily friendly and peace-loving, they administered harsh tortures and death to any who violated the privacy or sanctity of the priests and chiefs.

Welcomed by the friendly Hawaiian kings, the missionaries set about Americanizing the natives and making Hawaii an attractive land for further settlement. As the population grew and the island government became more stable, greater economic investment in the islands was made by people from the mainland. By 1852 Hawaii was ready to make its first of many appeals for statehood. Although the islands would not gain statehood for a century, they were annexed—much like Texas had been—in 1898.

By the time of the first statehood appeal, the work of missionaries and investors in Hawaiian fruit and sugar plantations showed in the urbanization of Honolulu and the building of stores, roads, churches, and other institutions of civilization. As had been true of settlers on the mainland, the white pioneers who settled in Hawaii were eager to introduce the trappings of the society back home as quickly as possible.

The Hawaiian frontier differed from other American frontiers only by its location in the middle of the ocean. In most other respects, the pattern of settlement in these islands reflected characteristics typical of the settlements along other lines of frontier.

Alaska
Even more than the story of Hawaii, the story of Alaska closely parallels the story of earlier settlement. In de-

veloping this state, natural resources have attracted settlers, Native Americans have been displaced, and the promise of new opportunities and great fortunes has lured prospectors and adventurers to the region. The harsh climate has forced the settlers to adapt old ways of life to new conditions. In these and many other ways, Alaska truly deserves the motto its citizens bear on their license plates: "The Last Frontier."

On October 18, 1867, the flag of Russia flew over Alaska for the last time. Since the late eighteenth century Alaska had been a thinly populated Russian colony. An exploring party sponsored by Peter the Great had traveled from Siberia to the lands across the thin finger of the Pacific separating Russia from North America. Vitus Bering led the expedition; the strait he crossed to reach America bears his name.

Bering's name was one of the few Russian legacies to Alaska. Overall, the Russians did little but deplete the area of fur-bearing animals. There were seldom more than five hundred Russians living in Alaska, and those people who did inhabit the snowy, icy land had no plans for permanent settlement. By the late 1850s, the Czar was badly in need of money. The Crimean War had taxed Russian resources, and it was clear that at any point aggressive North Americans—either from the United States or from Canada—could push into Russian America from the South.

It was the right time for Russia to sell this territory. In 1867 Secretary of State William Seward agreed to purchase Alaska on behalf of the United States. The price was $7.2 million. At the time many Americans derided the expenditure as a foolish waste. They called Alaska "Seward's Folly" and "Seward's Icebox." It would be nearly one hundred years before the continental United States would realize the vast riches that Seward had gained for the country.

Throughout the nineteenth century few Americans ventured into Alaska. There were plenty of frontier areas offering richer farmland and a more hospitable climate. Those few who were attracted to the region were drawn there by the same force that lured pioneers anywhere—the promise of fortunes to be made. In the nineteenth century fortunes could be made in Alaska in three ways—mining, plying the fur trade, and ice manufacture.

This last venture was the shortest lived. Until the acquisition of Alaska, people living in California got their ice from ships that carried the ice, packed in sawdust, all the way around Cape Horn from the eastern shore of the United States. California businessmen, however, had contracted with the Russians in Alaska for ice supplies as early as the 1850s. With the change in Alaska's ownership, Americans rushed to be part of the lucrative ice business. For twenty years, until the invention of machines that could manufacture ice, the Alaskan ice business flourished.

The greatest source of wealth in the early years of American Alaska was not ice. It was fur. Like earlier pioneers in the area of the lower forty-eight states, the first wave of adventurers into the new territory came to exploit the natural endowments of the region. By the 1860s the highly valued sea otter was all but extinct, but the fur seal remained in abundance. In time the fur seal, too, would face extinction, but at first the federal government took unprecedented steps to insure the continuation of the seals. Legislation placed the trapping of seals under federal control. This was a welcome change from the laissez-faire policy that had enabled white hunters to decimate the buffalo herds, often just for fun.

The legislation controlling seal trapping contained

another unusual provision that separates the history of Alaska's development from that of other areas with Native American populations. By law, any fur company operating in the rich fur-seal breeding grounds of the Pribilof Islands had to hire the native Aleutian Indians to work for them. The early fur traders in the Old Northwest and, subsequently, in the Rocky Mountains, had usually enjoyed good relations with the Indians, but this was the first time that an Indian group had received government protection right from the start.

Gold was the third possibility for wealth in the early years of Alaska. Between 1880 and 1900, prospectors in Alaska mined nearly twenty million dollars worth of gold. This mining activity stimulated what little population growth the territory enjoyed in the nineteenth century. The great Klondike strike of the 1890s caused the population of Alaska to double between 1890 and 1900, but the population remained stable at fewer than seventy-five thousand people from 1900 until 1940.

In the early years of Alaskan settlement, then, there were a number of similarities between this frontier and others. Because of its harsh climate and distance from other parts of the United States, however, Alaska did not attract the large numbers of farmers and trappers that other western regions had. Alaska's true frontier days came after World War II. Just as the Great Plains had blossomed with the advent of the railroad, the development of Alaska was greatly aided by automobiles and airplanes.

Since 1940 Alaska has undergone the stages of development that are associated with the growth of other frontier areas. Between 1940 and the 1980s, Alaskan cities grew, new businesses were started, and people began to settle permanently with their families in the territory. As had been true in other places, this settle-

The discovery of gold in the Klondike brought rapid development to Alaskan towns such as Juneau, shown here around the turn of the century.

ment was accompanied by boosterism—campaigns to attract more citizens through promises of money to be made, land almost free for the taking and a new start for anyone with a sense of adventure. The development culminated, as had the development of so many territories farther south, in the acceptance of Alaska as the forty-ninth state in 1959.

Instead of gold, the priceless treasure stimulating the growth of twentieth-century Alaska was oil. Instead of the hardships of the Oregon Trail, the pipeline pioneers are challenged by the hazards of the $1.4 million "Hickel Highway," an ice road over which supplies must be trucked to the oil fields around Prudhoe Bay. Truckers drive eighteen hours a day and leave their trucks running all night so that the engines do not freeze when the temperatures plummet to $-50°F$ and lower. The traditional hunting grounds of the Eskimos around Prudhoe Bay have been threatened, not by cattle drives and barbed wire this time, but by oil rigs.

The dealings between the federal government and the Eskimos highlight the lessons that the United States has learned about the injustice of violating native rights. In 1971, in order to pave the way for oil production on the North Slope, Congress agreed to give the Alaskan natives forty million acres of land and $962.5 million. (It is interesting to compare this figure to the total amount of money paid by the federal government to all Indians in the forty-eight continental states. From 1607 to 1971 they received about $250 million.)

The federal government has not only learned greater wisdom in dealing with native Americans on this latest frontier. The government has also become much wiser in its land policies. Throughout the nineteenth century, the government dispensed land as quickly as possible. A basic tenet of American freedom from the time of the Pilgrims to the signing of the Constitution to the construction of the transcontinental railroad had been the right of private individuals to develop land for their own use without government intervention. Ironically, coupled with this belief was the idea that the government should help both individuals and corporations with generous, no-strings-attached handouts of federal lands. What worked theoretically for small farmers was abused by large businesses and speculators right from the beginning. Many twentieth-century problems, including pollution, overcrowding, and soil erosion, are partly the results of the government's laissez-faire land policy.

With the opening of Alaska, the United States has truly run out of conventional frontiers. If the country is to maintain the wilderness area so important to its national heritage and sense of well-being, the lands of Alaska must be protected from uncontrolled exploitation. The beautiful scenery and rich wildlife of Alaska must be preserved for the public. The government has already taken steps in this direction. In 1971 eighty million acres were placed under permanent federal control. The "last frontier" should be there for many years to come. Visitors to Alaska will not only see the unique beauties of that state, but should also be able to recapture some feeling for the years of westward expansion when uninhabited land stretched for miles ahead of the pioneers.

9 *The Frontier Legacy Continues*

From the beginning of this nation's history, there was a tendency for people to move west as each succeeding generation sought new opportunities and new land. During the one hundred years following the ratification of the Constitution, most people in the country believed that the future of the United States lay in civilizing the frontier areas as rapidly as possible. Population growth, urbanization, faster transportation, and more efficient communication were all goals shared by early Americans as they sought to turn the wilderness into civilization. An anonymous pioneer diarist expressed the nation's sentiments when he wrote:

> When the solitary waste is peopled and convenient habitations arise amidst the former retreats of wild beasts; when the silence of nature is succeeded by the buzz of employment, the congratulations of society, and the voice of joy; in fine, when you behold competence and plenty springing from the bosom of dreary forests—what a lesson is afforded of the benevolent intention of Providence.

This diary entry was written in 1803. For the rest of the nineteenth century, the diarist's fellow citizens would people "the solitary waste" and fill the silence of the forest with "the buzz of employment." While doing so, they would reinforce in the minds of the nation and the rest of the world an image of Americans as adventuresome, hardworking, progressive, free, individualistic, and aggressive. At the same time, westward-moving Americans might have been characterized as materialistic, racist, and wasteful of the nation's resources. This negative side of westward expansion has predominated since the middle of the twentieth century. With little land left to explore, the United States has been left to wonder about the wisdom of eighteenth- and nineteenth-century habits and policies. The federal government during those two hundred years gave away far too much land, it has been argued. True, the nation urbanized and industrialized at a phenomenal rate, but was the cost too great? Pollution and a national unwillingness to conserve natural resources seem as much a part of the legacy of westward expansion as do freedom and progress.

The Sun Belt
The movement of American citizens into the Sun Belt is a twentieth-century development with direct ties to the frontier behavior of earlier centuries. Unlike Alaska and other earlier frontiers, however, the Sun Belt is not an undeveloped area. People are attracted to the states of the South and Southwest for several reasons. Some are tangible and some are intangible. Climate and new jobs are the tangible factors. The intangible factor is a legacy from the nation's early days, a sense that the West offers new hope, new beginnings, and as always, fortunes to be made. Where people are attracted to older regions of the Southeast, also Sun Belt areas, it can be said that they are heirs to the pioneer wanderlust that kept people on the move, even though the places they now seek may already be fully inhabited.

The movement to the Sun Belt areas got a boost from the federal government when President Jimmy Carter established a commission to draw up a "National Agenda for the '80s." This commission drew on the historical tradition of westward expansion to lend its support to the latest trend in that expansion, the movement of many thousands of people from the Northeastern and Midwestern states (nicknamed the "Frost Belt") to the Sun Belt areas of the South and Southwest. Between 1960 and 1980 cities in these regions experienced phenomenal growth. As had always been the case, people moved in order to find new economic opportunities.

Austin, Texas, is a good example of a Sun Belt city. Until the 1960s Austin was a small city with a stable population dependent on two businesses—the state university and the state government offices. Early in the 1960s, however, Austin's citizens began to advertise its attractive tax structure and climate. Northeastern businesses recognized the advantages of relocating in Austin and the boom was on.

This kind of population boom in Sun Belt areas differs significantly from earlier migrations. First, people moving to the Sun Belt are moving to already established urban areas. Second, a large percentage of the people moving to these areas are impoverished immigrants. Earlier in the nation's history, many western travelers came from the wealthier segments of the immigrant population, if they were immigrants at all. People making the trek west had generally been people of some financial resources.

Unfortunately the new migration resembles older western movements in its exploitation of natural resources. Air pollution and water shortages plague the Sun Belt cities. In the 1960s and 1970s little urban planning took place as cities boomed; more was better, and the consequences could be counted later. In Los Angeles, California; Phoenix, Arizona; and Miami, Florida, burgeoning populations were a source of city pride during these decades. Numbers meant success in much the same way that population growth had meant survival one hundred years earlier for such communities as Denver, Colorado; San Francisco, California; and Virginia City, Nevada.

The urban sprawl in the Sun Belt failed to take into consideration the dangerously low water tables in the region. Water shortages are chronic and threaten to become worse. Inadequate public transportation in many of the region's cities necessitates private automobile ownership. Traffic clogs the streets and pollution clogs the air. Sun Belt states are calling for the assistance of the federal government to help with the problems brought on by the new migration. If the federal government complies, it will not be the first time that the aid of the central government has been enlisted to help solve problems created by expansion. Protection from Indians, improved roads, canal and railroad construction are examples of earlier demands that were met by federal assistance.

There may have been no "frontier line" after the census of 1890, but the Sun Belt is ample evidence that frontiers—new areas to which people migrate in substantial numbers in order to make their fortunes—are still very much in existence. These new frontiers share some of the older traditions, but have other characteristics that are solely their own. It is safe to say, however, that in no other nation has opportunity been so closely linked to migration and to starting a new life in a new area. That is uniquely the American tradition of westward expansion.

The Heritage of the Frontier

In today's America, the heritage of westward expansion is recalled in many ways. For example, there is the "back-to-the-land" movement that has attracted some young people and media attention since the 1960s. These late twentieth-century pioneers attempt to find farms in remote areas where they can escape civilization. They want to rear their families in ways similar to those they believe their ancestors used on the frontier. These people are motivated by their sense of history, but they have not learned the end of the story. Their ancestors did not wish to remain on the edges of civilization. Rather, they settled in remote areas, hoping to stretch civilization that much farther.

Violence in modern American life is also often attributed to the nation's western heritage. The right of private citizens to own all kinds of firearms is a privilege adopted in times of frontier necessity. No other nation in western civilization has a similar tradition of gun ownership. When homeowners shoot burglars during robbery attempts, there are usually vocal citizens who defend people's right to defend their property with guns. They place the gun-toting homeowner squarely within the tradition of frontier justice, where local citizens made the law. Modern America, however, is not removed from police and courts. The continuation of this tradition of individual "justice," long after the original need has disappeared, may account in large part for the nation's high rate of gunshot wounds and gun deaths.

In some ways the influence of westward expansion remains much the same as it always has. The western states remain a real force in politics and are likely to grow even stronger as the population of the Sun Belt increases. (Ronald Reagan is a western president who borrows liberally from the images of the frontier when he poses in his cowboy hat astride his horse on his California ranch.)

Frederick Jackson Turner perhaps overstated the case when he asserted that the presence of an advancing line of frontier best explained the nation's history. However, he was not wrong at all in emphasizing the importance of the frontier as a major factor in the development of the United States. Whatever the flaws in Turner's argument, it should be clear to any student of American history that western expansion has been a unique and significant force in the nation's growth.

Suggestions for Further Reading

The history of western expansion has been treated thoroughly by historians since Turner, but anyone reading about western history would be remiss in ignoring Frederick Jackson Turner's essay "The Significance of the Frontier in American History." Originally published in the 1890s, it is handily available in a variety of essay collections, among them, Frederick J. Turner, *The Frontier in American History* (Krieger, 1976).

Other major works that are both readable and comprehensive include Frederic L. Paxson, *History of the American Frontier* (Houghton Mifflin, 1964), Robert Reigel, *America Moves West* (Holt, 1956), William K. Wyant, *Westward in Eden* (University of California Press, 1982) and Frederick Merk, *History of the Westward Movement* (Knopf, 1978). Ray A. Billington is perhaps the most famous, and certainly the most prolific, of modern writers on the subject. His one volume, *The Westward Movement in the United States* (Van Nostrand, 1959), contains not only a brief survey of the history of western migration, but also a good sampling of documents representing various stages of the move west. Another good collection of primary sources can be found in *Eye-Witnesses to Wagon Trains West* (Charles Scribner's Sons, 1973) by James Hewitt. Harvey Carter's *Far Western Frontiers* (American Historical Association, 1972) is valuable for his essays as well as for his bibliographic notes.

Various historians have written about specific geographic aspects of the movement west. In *The Last West: A History of the Great Plains of North America* (Thomas Crowell, 1974), Russell McKee writes of the settling of the Great Plains and in *Mining Frontier: Contemporary*

Accounts from the American West in the 19th Century (University of Oklahoma Press, 1967), Marvin Louis writes of the great gold, silver, and copper strikes of the 1870s and 1880s. Bernard DeVoto's *Across the Wide Missouri* (Crown, 1947) remains the single best volume on the Rocky Mountain fur trade.

Other historians have chosen to focus on specific groups of people important to the westward movement. Often these works are attempts to correct earlier generalizations by concentrating on parts of the population who may not fit the general categories. Three excellent works on women on the frontier are Annette Kolodny, *The Land Before Her* (University of North Carolina Press, 1984), Julie Roy Jeffrey, *Frontier Women: The Trans-Mississippi West, 1840–1880* (Hill and Wang, 1979), and Sandra Myres, *Westering Women* (University of New Mexico Press, 1982). Kenneth Libo and Irving Howe have recently contributed a richly illustrated history of the Jewish western experience, *We Lived There, Too* (St. Martin, 1984). William W. Savage, Jr. has examined the myth and reality of the cowboy's west in *The Cowboy Hero: His Image in American History and Culture* (University of Oklahoma Press, 1979). Philip Dunham and Everett L. Jones offer an interesting account of black cowboys in *The Negro Cowboys* (Dodd, Mead, 1965). Although this work has been challenged for erroneous statistics, it remains the most comprehensive and accurate study of the minority experience on the range. Roger D. McGrath has studied the extent of violence in western towns. The result in his book, *Gunfighters, Highwaymen and Vigilantes: Violence on the Frontier* (University of California Press, 1984).

Whether one's interest in western history is general or specific, the literature is rich, entertaining, and informative.

Index

Adams, Alexander B., 95, 105
Adams, John, 33
Adams, John Quincy, 12, 81
Agricultural revolution, 116–118
Alabama, 20, 36, 46, 48
Alaska, 15, 126–132
American Revolution, 23–26, 32
Appalachians, 23–25
Arizona, 100, 135
Arkansas, 39
Articles of Confederation, 27
Austin, Moses, 52
Austin, Stephen, 52
Austin, Texas, 135

"Back-to-the-land" movement, 137
Bacon, Nathaniel, 24
Bacon's Rebellion, 24
Bering, Vitus, 127
Bidwell, John, 56
Billington, Ray A., 30, 39, 102, 118
Billy the Kid, 113
Boone, Daniel, 19, 25–27, 40, 120, 122
Bridger, Jim, 40–41, 116
Brown, John, 75
Buchanan, James, 55
Buffalo, New York, 30, 49
Burnett, Peter, 56
Bush, Vannevar, 12–13

Calamity Jane, 19, 111
Calhoun, John C., 70–72, 82
California, 20, 53, 58–61, 63, 69, 70, 72, 99–100, 102, 135, 136
Capitalism, 14
Carolinas, 24, 25, 27, 63–64, 70, 78

Carson, Kit, 19, 40–42, 58, 116
Carter, Harvey L., 53, 100, 107
Carter, Jimmy, 134
Cather, Willa, 122
Cattle, 108–111
Census of 1890, 13, 14
Characteristics of pioneers, 18–20, 26, 43
Chief Joseph, 87
Chinese immigrants, 92
Cincinnati, 49, 50
Cities, 49–51
Civil War, 63, 68, 78, 86–87
Clark, William, 40
Clay, Henry, 70–72, 83–84
Cleveland, Grover, 122
Colorado, 20, 39, 60, 100, 107, 110, 113, 136
Compromise of 1850, 71–72, 74
Computers, 15
Connecticut, 27, 29
Constitution, 14
Copper, 100, 107
Coronado, Vasquez de, 115
Cotton, 36–37
Cowboys, 12, 87, 99, 108–113, 120
Crèvecoeur, Jean de, 11, 13
Custer's Last Stand, 87

Dakotas, 39
Dawes Act (1887), 88–89
Democracy, 14, 19, 48–49
Democratic-Republicans, 33
Discrimination. *See* Prejudice and discrimination
Donner Party, 57–58
Douglas, Stephen A., 51–52, 73–74, 76, 77
Dutcher, Flora, 119

Earp, Wyatt, 111
English laws, 14
Eskimos, 129, 131

Federalists, 33
Five Civilized Tribes, 38–39, 82, 83, 88
Florida, 81, 82, 135
Free Soil Party, 75
Frémont, Jessie Benton, 58
Frémont, John Charles, 58, 122
Fulton, Robert, 45
Fur traders, 40–41, 43, 128–129

Gadsden, James, 60
Gadsden Purchase of 1854, 60
Gardner, Charles, 41
Garland, Hamlin, 122
Georgia, 27, 81, 83
German immigrants, 90
Geronimo, 87
Glidden, Joseph, 120
Gold, 59, 60–61, 69–70, 99–100, 102–104, 129, 130
Goldwater, Barry, 91
Goldwater, Mike, 91
Great Plains, 20, 86–89, 115–124
Greeley, Horace, 18
Guest, Edgar, 20
Guggenheim, Meyer, 91

Hadley, Massachusetts, 26
Harrison, William H., 34, 37–38, 45
Hawaii, 125–126
Hewitt, James, 56–57
Hickok, Wild Bill, 113
Homestead Act (1862), 105, 106, 117, 118
Howe, Irving, 91

Idaho, 100, 107
Illinois, 20, 36, 47, 94, 95
Immigrants, 90–93
Indian Removal Act (1830), 84

Indiana, 36, 47, 48, 51
Indians, 12, 18–19, 26, 33–35, 37–39, 54, 55, 58, 73, 79–90, 115, 116, 122, 124, 129, 131
Iowa, 39
Irish immigrants, 20, 90

Jackson, Andrew, 38–39, 45, 63–65, 81, 82, 84
Jacksonian democracy, 63–65
James Brothers, 113
Jay, John, 33
Jay Treaty (1794), 33
Jefferson, Thomas, 28, 33, 34, 39–40
Jeffrey, Julie Roy, 107
Jewish pioneers, 91

Kansas, 39, 74–75, 110
Kansas-Nebraska Territory, 73–75
Kennedy, John F., 125
Kentucky, 12, 20, 25–27, 34, 46, 47, 51
Klondike, 129, 130

Land Acts (1800, 1804, and 1820), 47
Land Ordinance of 1785, 28–29
Land Ordinance of 1787, 31–32
Land sales, 28–30, 46–47, 117–118
Lee, Jason, 54
Leutz, Emmanuel, 17
Lewis, Meriwether, 40
Libo, Kenneth, 91
Lincoln, Abraham, 66, 68, 75–78
Lincoln, Mary Todd, 77
Lincoln, Tom, 20, 77
Lindneux, Robert, 85
Little Bighorn, 87
Louis, Marvin, 102
Louisiana, 39, 46, 48
Louisiana Purchase, 39–40, 48, 69, 74
Luther Standing Bear, 18–19

Mail, 103, 105
Maine, 24
Manifest destiny, 51–53, 78
Marshall, James, 60, 99
Mason, Richard B., 60
Massachusetts, 24, 27, 68
McGrath, Roger D., 111, 113
McKee, Russell, 115, 116
Merk, Frederick, 72, 94
Mexico, 52–53, 59–60, 65–69
Mining, 99–100, 102–104, 106–107, 129, 130
Missionaries, 54
Mississippi, 36, 46, 48
Missouri, 39, 40, 48, 94–95
Montana, 39, 100
Morison, Samuel Eliot, 83
Mormons, 93–97
Morrill Land Grant Act (1862), 118
Morris, Esther, 107

Napoleon Bonaparte, 39
Native Americans. *See* Indians
Nebraska, 39, 74–75, 110
Nevada, 20, 59, 61, 100, 102, 113, 136
New Mexico, 59, 60
New Orleans, 36, 48
New York, 24, 27
Northwest Ordinance, 31–32

Oakley, Annie, 15
Ohio, 12, 27–31, 46, 47, 51
Oil, 131
Oklahoma, 39, 122–124
Old Northwest Territory, 28, 31–33, 37
Oregon Territory, 53–58
Oregon Trail, 54, 56
O'Sullivan, John L., 51, 52

Paxson, Frederic L., 82, 83
Paxton Boys, 25
Pennsylvania, 25

Pike, Albert, 41
Pinckney's Treaty (1795), 36
Pittsburgh, 20, 25
Polk, James, 59, 66, 68
Pollution, 134–136
Polygamy, 94, 97
Population, 15–16, 36, 45–48
Pottawatomie Massacre, 75
Preemption, 28
Prejudice and discrimination, 18, 78–97, 107
Primogeniture, 28
Proclamation of 1763, 25
Prophet, The, 38

Railroads, 20, 69–70, 73–74, 77, 86–87, 105–106, 118
Ranching, 108–111, 120
Reagan, Ronald, 137
Reed, Elizabeth, 58
Regulators, 25
Religion, 52–53, 54
Reservations, 81, 87–89
Revere, Joseph, 102
Ride, Sally, 15
Riegel, Robert, 20, 34
Rolvaag, O. E., 122

San Francisco, 102
Savage, William W., Jr., 111
Scandinavian immigrants, 20, 92–93
Seward, William, 127
Silver, 61, 100, 107
Sioux Wars of 1890, 87–88
Sitting Bull, 87
Slavery, 49, 66, 69–72, 74–75, 79
Smith, Joseph, 93–94
Sod houses, 119, 121
"Sooners," 122
Southwest Territory, 36–39, 48–49
Space exploration, 15
Spalding, Eliza, 54
Spalding, Henry, 54

Speculation, 29–30
Starr, Belle, 113
States' rights, 70–71
Steamboat, 45
Strauss, Levi, 91
Sun Belt, 134–136

Taylor, Zachary, 67, 70, 72
Tecumseh, 38, 80
Tennessee, 27, 34, 46, 47, 51, 64
Territorial government, 31–32
Texas, 52–53, 59, 66, 108, 110
Thoreau, Henry David, 12, 66
Transportation, 45, 103, 105–106
Treaty of Greenville, 34–35, 37
Treaty of Guadalupe Hidalgo, 59, 68–69
Treaty of Paris, 23, 33
Turner, Frederick Jackson, 13–14, 21, 48, 72, 88, 92, 138
Twain, Mark, 91

Utah, 59, 95, 97

Vermont, 34
Virginia, 24, 27, 40

War of 1812, 37–39, 63
Webster, Daniel, 70–72
Western Reserve, 29
Whitman, Marcus, 54–55, 81
Whitman, Narcissa, 54–55, 81
Whitman, Walt, 12, 19
Wisconsin, 92–93
Wister, Owen, 99
Women, 54, 107, 111, 117–118
Wounded Knee, Battle of, 87–88
Wyant, William K., 15
Wyoming, 39, 60, 107

Young, Brigham, 94–95